Miracles in the Jungle

*Memoirs of a Missionary Family
in
Papua New Guinea*

David Rogne

Copyright © 2010 by David Rogne

Miracles in the Jungle
by David Rogne

Printed in the United States of America

ISBN 9781609573058

All rights reserved solely by the author. The author guarantees all contents are original and do not infringe upon the legal rights of any other person or work. No part of this book may be reproduced in any form without the permission of the author. The views expressed in this book are not necessarily those of the publisher.

Unless otherwise indicated, Bible quotations are taken from the New King James Version of the Bible. Copyright © 1982 by Thomas Nelson, Inc.

www.xulonpress.com

Table of Contents

Preface vii

Introduction ix

1   Tsobu: The Last to Hear 11

2   Tsobu: Delays 21

3   Tsobu: The Hike Up 27

4   Tsobu: Twenty-six Pass From Death to Life! 34

5   Tsobu: Back Home 42

6   Gail's Trial 50

7   Schultze 57

8   Ifisyu 64

9   What is a Missionary? 72

10   The Art of Language Learning 78

11   The Gospel 85

Preface

My purpose in writing this book is to reveal the many miraculous things that God did in our lives. He called us into His family. He equipped us to be able to share His message with others. And He sent us out as missionaries to a foreign land. He promised to be with us. It was a promise He certainly kept!

My desire is that other believers will see that when God calls you to something that may seem frightening or insurmountable, it is definitely the right choice to obey Him and hang on for the ride! We've seen God do the miraculous many times and it has strengthened our faith in Him and deepened our love for Him.

If God is prompting you to go out on a limb then take that step of faith and, no matter what, keep your eyes fixed on Him! He calls us to things that seem impossible, and that's the way it should be. He *must* get the glory. It is in His strength we go, not our own!

In that spirit, I dedicate this book to the people of God everywhere in this world who have been called to Him and who love Him with all their hearts.

So if you are in the trenches laboring for Christ – **be encouraged**, keep on keeping on. And to those of you wishing for the courage to take that leap of faith, I say**, "Jump – Go big or stay home!!!"**

There is no greater joy than to serve The Author of Life!

Introduction

We were sent out by our local churches to the island nation of Papua New Guinea in January 1998. Jonathan was two and a half years old and Seth a mere 10 months! Baby Seth was admired by the native ladies as he was so big and chubby and fair, they absolutely adored his fat cheeks and long blonde hair. Jonathan became a hit with all the missionary kids on base due to his ability to lead them out every morning, broom in hand, in the quest to discover new bug species!

We traveled from Spokane to Seattle to Los Angeles to Vancouver to Sydney to Brisbane to Cairns to Port Moresby to Goroka to Wewak to Hayfield and then drove the last few miles down a pot holed dirt road to Maprik. It was there that we spent the first 10 months in PNG learning language and culture. We then were privileged to spend time in two separate tribal locations working with the young believers, and we also helped in two support roles – supply buying and running the mission guest house.

Following are some of the things that happened to us as we endeavored to give our lives to reach out to the people in PNG. In these pages you will be able to live those first three years with us as we encounter a village chief intent on murder and payback, medical mishaps and miracles, a killer hike, snakes, spiders, centipedes and millipedes, demonic attacks, and people who trusted God through great trials.

One last disclaimer and we'll begin: much of missionary work is just that —WORK. In this text you will be privy to a few of the adventures that we lived through, but I have not described the real day-in day-out life of the missionary for you. Besides, every missionary is different and our experience may be worlds apart from a missionary near you! So sit back, grab a favorite beverage or snack and enjoy!

1 Tsobu: The Last to Hear

If any man wants to follow after Me, let him first count the cost.
– Yeshua

Beginnings

As a boy I loved to listen to the missionaries who would come to our small Baptist church and thrill our hearts with stories of adventure in reaching the lost. The normal church meetings sometimes became monotonous to us children, but there were three things that never seemed to get boring. First, potlucks. Who isn't having a good time when they're eating? It's nearly impossible to ruin the coming together for food and fellowship. We children would eat desert until our stomachs ached then run off to play outside, while the adults talked for hours solving all the world's problems. Second, the singing. A witch once told me that the thing she hated the most about us Christians is our singing. But the joy of the Lord is our strength! The more you love the Lord the more you enjoy singing His praises. I suppose that is why the fellowships that really love the Lord sing the loudest! Have you ever been to a fundamental, temperamental, right-wing, on-fire, Baptist church? Only the preaching will keep you from thinking you ended up with a group of Pentecostals! And last but not least, the guest speakers. Why is it so much fun hearing the views and stories of others you rarely see? For me, the missionaries who had been to the jungle had the best stories. They boldly endured dangerous encounters with huge snakes and other such critters in their efforts to take the gospel to the ends of the earth. And they had lived to tell about it!

So growing up, I always dreamed of the day when I would be sent out in the Lord's will. No paved roads for me, I wanted to go where Christ had not yet been preached.

My first stateside "missionary" trip was in 1986. Our high school youth group from Valley Fourth Memorial Church in Spokane, Washington, was invited to share one month of our lives with the children on an Indian reservation. We traveled in an old school bus for several days up into the northern half of British Columbia, Canada. We conducted Five Day Clubs and other fun activities for the young children. The older kids would come nightly and play games with us. After expending some energy, we would have a good feed before gathering around to listen to a speaker. There were opportunities for us to share our testimonies and we saw several people put their trust in Jesus Christ. It was a unique experience that helped put the love of ministry in my life. We all made a lot of friends that summer. One of my friends loved to ride bucking broncos. I had such a yearning to participate in the activities around me that I asked to ride in the upcoming rodeo. My leaders did not allow this, for reasons I can now understand! Between teaching the Bible, playing games with the children, and spending time one-on-one with the local people, the passion for missionary life took firm root in my heart. I wanted to serve the Lord forever.

Papua New Guinea

During the next twelve years, I grew in my walk with the Lord, graduated from Spokane Bible College (Moody Northwest), completed three years of training with New Tribes Mission, got married, and started a family! In January 1998, my wife Gail and I and our two sons were living outside a remote town in Papua New Guinea called Maprik, taking the language and culture orientation course, learning the trade language of Melanesian Tok Pidgin. That's when a very special invitation was offered to me.

Miracles in the Jungle

"Maprik woman with firewood"

To the farthest and last village

But first a little bit of history on this place called Tsobu where I was to go — Bob and another missionary, we'll call him George, had teamed up to bring the gospel to a remote tribe living in the Sepik River region of Papua New Guinea. That was back in the late 70's, it was now 1998. It had taken them years to learn the language and preach the gospel. It was a daunting task, plus both of these men had responsibilities in field leadership, all the while raising their families. Not to mention the endless hours of laboring to translate the Bible into the tribal language, and the task of teaching the people to read and write their language. Did I mention working with the local believers to get them grounded in the Word? Or maybe I forgot to tell you of the efforts to coordinate the teams of native missionary men sent out to take the gospel to the outlying villages. Of course there are problems to iron out wherever there are people involved, and that meant that Bob and George needed to work with the other groups of believers as they matured as well! Oh yeah, then there is the problem of life — you know, the constant ebb and flow of kids growing up and needing their parents, the various medical issues that seem to happen to every family, and so on.

To be truthful, it takes a special work of the Lord to accomplish the hundreds of tasks that are required to see a tribe completely evangelized. By "evangelized" I mean that <u>all</u> the villages in the tribal group have had the chance to hear the gospel proclaimed to them in their own language.

In a nutshell, someone has to learn the language, create an orthography (an alphabet to represent each speech sound), translate the Bible, teach the Word of God from start to finish, teach the people to read and write their own language, and then ordain men mature enough to lead the flock of God who can then send out other qualified men to go spread the Word to other villages that have not yet heard! Does this sound easy to you?!

So when this veteran missionary Bob invited me to go with him to proclaim the gospel to the very last village in his language group, I was elated! We were to meet at his base called Bisorio, where the airstrip and missionary houses were. Teaming up with us was a group of mature believers who were some of Bob's original converts. They would spend about six months in a remote place called Tsobu, teaching through the Bible chronologically so that the people could understand the whole story start to finish.

Tsobu was far away. Bob had made the journey once before, but not without casualties! You see, hiking through the jungle can be dangerous and is a bit hard on one's clothing — and maybe even on the body inside the clothing! Bob had experienced a severe blowout with his only pair of shoes. For several difficult days, he struggled

Miracles in the Jungle

along with vines wrapped around his feet in an attempt to hold together what was left of his shoes! He told me emphatically, "Bring two pairs of hiking shoes in good condition!" I proudly thought of the new generation of Nike hiking boots that I was just itching to try out and was confident *I would not need* a second pair. Boy, I am sure glad I heeded the wisdom of Jungle Bob and brought a back-up pair!

"Bisorio bushmen"

Opposition!

As the days approached for the trip to begin, I found myself distracted from the day to day chores of language learning and other tasks now so tedious to me. All I could think about was hiking through the jungle with the brave natives, living the adventures, killing snakes of mammoth proportions, and maybe even spotting some rare creature unknown to science. My daydreams were shattered, however, when the night before I was to fly out to Bisorio, my oldest son almost died.

Have you ever gotten the feeling that someone (like our enemy) doesn't appreciate what you're doing?

I had experienced this same feeling of resistance a few years back in 1995 during my month-long survey trip to PNG. I had flown to a tribe deep in the Sepik region to spend a few days with the missionaries there. The heat in the jungle is oppressive. So after my work was completed, I headed across the airstrip to the river to join the other guys already cooling off. The sky was clear and glorious and the grass incredibly green. I was all alone with not a soul in sight, when all of a sudden a presence enveloped me. The feeling was absolutely intense. Every hair on my body bristled. This presence was seething with hatred for me and I could feel its utter desire to kill me. I remember thinking, why would this demon be so disturbed by my being here, when I can't possibly be any threat — I don't even speak their language! I suppose the image of the One I serve was a painful reminder of the powerlessness of this being that now disturbed me. "I am a child of the Most High God," I declared out loud. The suffocating presence vanished immediately. I pondered this weird experience a moment. The God of the Bible truly is King over all the earth!

And now, something seemed to be trying to keep me from meeting up with Bob. It was as if someone didn't like us getting the village church leaders together to go preach the gospel in the last stronghold of the enemy. Was I just imagining all this? My thoughts were horribly interrupted by the seriousness of the situation in which I now found myself. I had told my two and a half year old son to go into his bedroom to have Gail get him ready for bed. It was a distance of maybe 30 feet. Instead, he had walked over to my dinner plate and somehow swallowed my Mefloquine (anti-malarial) tablet that Gail had left there.

The ironic thing is both our sons are usually very obedient. We have a zero disobedience policy at our house and it keeps everyone happy and doing the right thing! Also, Jonathan couldn't keep anything down that irritated his throat in the least; he had a very queasy stomach. But somehow he had managed to choke down a huge, bitter Mefloquine tablet — something that I struggled to do!

I ran to him and immediately tried to get him to throw it up. I stuck my finger down his throat and yelled to Gail to go get the older missionaries. She hurried to the house next door and asked them to come and help. A gravestone lay just behind their house belonging to another missionary's son who had died 10 years before (almost to the day) of the same thing (and this boy had been the same age as our Jonny). Charles came running and asked Gail to get some charcoal and a bottle of coke. We just couldn't get our son to throw up. It was a Sunday and he had just taken his own three malaria pills; every Sunday the boys took a special weekly dose. We frantically tried to get him to drink down the charcoal, but to no avail.

Someone called the mission headquarters and another requested an emergency flight with the doctor. Things were happening fast and these veteran missionaries were moving as if the little guy's life was on the line!

A report came back from headquarters that the doctor had contacted the Center for Disease Control in America. They explained that if the medication was not vomited up within 15 minutes then Jonny's heart would begin to slow down and eventually stop! We tried again to make him vomit. Absolutely nothing worked.

We got our son into the base utility truck and started down the dirt road for the airstrip. We prayed as we went. Gail had the foresight to bring some clothes and my backpack for our journey. I was just lost holding my little boy.

We all loaded into the mission plane and the doctor began immediately checking Jonny's pulse and listening to his heart. His pulse was weak and the heartbeat a bit slow. The twin-engine plane lifted off and ascended to cruising altitude. The doctor unbuckled and checked the toddler again. There was no question now, the drugs were stopping his heart for sure. We were going to lose our little boy. The doctor looked at me and shook his head. There was nothing he could do. I knelt beside my son and closed my tear-filled eyes. "Father, I told You that I gave You my life and You have control of all our lives. You have the right to take my son, he is Yours. But please, have pity on me. Save my little boy... I KNOW You can."

It is an amazing study when you reflect on all the people that Jesus healed in the Gospels — so many of them cried out to Him in desperation. There were the four men who trusted so strongly in the Savior's compassion and power that they took somebody's roof apart to lower their buddy down to Him (Mark 2:1-12). Another time, in Mark 10:46-52, a blind man, sensing the commotion, discovered that it was Jesus who was passing by and so he cried out loudly, "Jesus, Son of David, have mercy on me!" They couldn't shut the guy up. He cried out even more intensely, "Jesus, Son of David, have mercy on me!" How was it that this man could see so clearly who Jesus was, when so many of the scholarly and learned couldn't figure it out? In Luke 23:42, we are told of two thieves who hung on crosses on either side of Jesus. One of them thought only of temporary relief from his trouble. But the other man desired an eternal healing. "Jesus, remember me when You come into Your kingdom."

The scripture tells us, "the effective, <u>fervent</u> prayer of a righteous man avails much." (James 5:16b, emphasis added) It was like that there in the confines of the twin-engine Cessna. I cried out to the only One Who has the power to do anything for us at all — and He answered. Jonathan's eyes opened and strength immediately returned to his limp body. He was healed!!

The doctor was shocked. He couldn't believe what he was seeing. He checked the now very alive patient. I asked if we could go back. If God healed my boy, there was no longer a need for all this. NO WAY! The doctor insisted on taking Jonny to the main base to monitor him for 24 hours.

On one hand I was ecstatic to have my son back, but on the other hand I felt like Satan had won the battle. Now how would I get to meet up with Bob?

Goroka

When we arrived at the mission headquarters in Goroka, it was still bothering me that Satan had kept me from doing the very thing I'd come to PNG to do. I guess it shows how our wrong beliefs can dramatically affect the way we feel. If I would have believed the Word of God fully, I would not have felt so worked over by the devil.

Consider for instance a scripture that has come to mean so much to me. Psalm 37:23 says "The steps of a good man are ordered by the LORD, and He delights in his way." Or the verse that saved my life found in Ephesians 2:10, "For we are His workmanship, created in Christ Jesus for good works, which God prepared beforehand that we should walk in them." Is there anything that can ever happen to us that is beyond God's control?

"Your eyes saw my substance, being yet unformed. And in Your book they all were written, the days fashioned for me, when as yet there were none of them." (Psalm 139:16)

The next morning the sun shone brightly but I was still thinking about missing my opportunity of a lifetime. I was so very thankful that God had worked a miracle on our behalf. It is a truly amazing fact that the God who spoke the UNI-VERSE (single spoken sentence!) into existence actually loves us so much that He did the ultimate to bring us back to Himself. I thought about that. The God Who created all of this chose to pour out His love and grace upon me by inviting me to be His child and then sent me out to tell men living in darkness that their Creator wants them to be reunited with Him as His children as well! It's no wonder that He works such remarkable miracles in our lives. I decided to once again simply trust in Him and in His sovereign will for me. I was at peace and full of joy again!

As we were eating breakfast that morning, someone came to the screen door. "Hey, I just heard that a plane here is going to Bisorio in the Sepik region and there's 90 kilos of space left on the flight. Do you want to go?" I don't recall who it was that brought me the good news, but I remember wondering to myself the miracle of this. That flight had been planned possibly weeks in advance and I myself had known nothing of it. All I knew is that my pack plus my own weight came to 90 kilograms! God knew what He was doing! Instead of my going on a special flight from our orientation base, He had this planned for me before He created the earth! **Game on**! Satan lost that round and lost badly!!

2 Tsobu: Delays

"Be sober, be vigilant; because your adversary the devil walks about like a roaring lion, seeking whom he may devour. Resist him, steadfast in the faith..." 1 Peter 5:8,9a

Flying from the cooler Highlands down to the Sepik jungle, I reflected on the power and humor of my God. He had shown me His greatness in the midst of testing my heart, plus He provided for my wife and children. I didn't know exactly how long I would be gone but it could be several weeks. My wife needed the fellowship of other ladies there at the large base and the kids would have some fun playing with other youngsters. God is good — all the time!

When we approached Bisorio, the pilot skillfully looked over the airfield. It was soft. So much rain had fallen that the river was swollen and things would perhaps be a little bit muddy. It is my humble opinion that missionary jungle pilots are some of the best pilots in the world. Fly with them in dicey conditions and I'm sure that you'll come to the same conclusion! Upon touching down, the wheels sank into the runway a few inches but the pilot maneuvered the aircraft brilliantly. I was so thankful that God had given us the very best pilots. Bob assured him that we would fill in the ruts as soon as he left.

Bob had spent many years in this place and it was a challenge to maintain everything. I looked around and decided to do all I could to fix the solar electric system while I was there. I had some good training in that area and was eager to bless the "old school" missionary with a more updated approach to solar systems!

Bob and I had great fun working at various projects while we waited for the day that we could get started on our hike. But every day seemed to bring more delays.

Constrictor

Not only had the disaster with my son occurred, but here in Bisorio, the wife of a church elder had been attacked by a huge snake on the way to her garden. The serpent struck, pulling her to the ground. It then started swallowing her leg. She screamed frantically, yelling for help. Men came running and tried to pull the beastly thing off her leg. But it had sharp teeth that shredded the muscles as it fought to hang on. She survived but her leg was severely damaged from the attack.

There are three unusual things about this. First, python type constrictors rarely, if ever, start with the feet; they first suffocate their victim with bone crushing force and then consume it headfirst. Second, they don't usually attempt to eat something that is not yet dead. And third, most of the pythons and boas in New Guinea don't get large enough to eat grown adults.

Many saw this as an attack of the enemy to keep us from going to Tsobu.

Another thing that happened was most of the elders suddenly came down with a strange sickness. We prayed for them, and little by little they recovered. But talk was going around that the spirit Denaya was behind all this.

The demon Denaya

Bob, George, and the mature tribal Christians had been successful in taking the gospel message to all but one of the hamlets in their language group. This last mountain village of Tsobu was a great distance away and very difficult to get to. Bob had made the journey once before. Some time after this, a spirit had appeared in the form of a blue cloud to the people of this place. This entity called itself "Denaya" and had made a deal with the people. It promised to hold pigs on the trail for them to kill and eat and to help them with their enemies, IF they would adopt his new language and live inside his fence. This fence he commanded them to build around the place we called Tsobu. Oh yeah, and they were NEVER to listen to a missionary or any other Christian. They must follow Denaya only!

One may scoff and say, "I don't believe in spirits" or "I don't believe in God" but that does not in any way keep them from existing!

When Gail and I returned to America we discovered this postmodern notion of relativism – the idea that your truth is true for you and my truth is true for me. We heard of people claiming they could create their own reality. It's utter nonsense. Think about a bullet coming out of the barrel of a gun. It doesn't need to have someone believe in it to be real. Someone who thinks that they are the god of their own universe is someone who is simply delusional! **Newsflash**… believing you can fly will not make it so. Were you to jump off a cliff, you would fall. Belief in the TRUTH is what is required. The One in Whom I believe has the power to speak the world into existence. That is a fact. He loved us so much that He died for us in the person of His only begotten Son, Yeshua. That is a fact. You can choose to believe or to not believe, but facts are stubborn things!

Another Attack!

So this entity, it would seem, was performing some unusual disturbances to keep us from bringing the gospel up to those people "living inside his fence." I wish that I had been a bit more diligent in recording all the ways he was trying to thwart our efforts, but alas I have forgotten many of them. One I can recount for you, however, is a close call Bob and I had with a bolt of lightning.

The two of us were washing the evening dishes. It was again raining and Bob and I were chatting away merrily. Bob is the type of guy that makes you want to be around him. He is so gifted in being able to speak with anyone and make it fun. We were standing there in his little jungle house with the kitchen window screen just a foot or two in front of us. All of a sudden a bolt of lightning struck the radio antennae pole attached to the outside edge of the window. The flash was blinding and the noise deafening.

As I came to my senses, I found myself on the floor with Bob laughing heartily at me.

"You should have seen yourself jump!" he chided. "You were so scared you collapsed to the floor!" It took me a second or two to register what he had said, and then I realized that he as well was lying on the floor. "Just where do you think you are, Bob?" I shot back, laughing at the long, skinny man laying only four feet away.

We started looking around the place, inspecting the damage. The radio antennae was shot with the co-ax in the middle blown out completely. A long black burn mark snaked its way across the linoleum floor. The refrigerator wasn't working and many other electrical items were blown out.

"Hey, listen, Dave," Bob held up a hand, his head tilted to one side, "I think I hear the generator running."

I paused, and sure enough, the sound of a diesel engine could be heard over the din of the pouring rain pounding down on the metal roof.

As we suspected, the generator, some 50 yards away, had somehow been started by the spike of current from the lightning. When we went out to the gennie shed to investigate, we found the wiring was completely fried. We pulled the lever back that closed the fuel shut-off valve. With no more fuel, the engine chugged to a halt.

The more we looked around, the more we realized it was time to go. A bully preys on someone who won't fight back. Maybe you've heard it said that the best defense is a great offense. Bob and I prayed that night that God would put a stop to the enemy's work and open up a way for us to leave for Tsobu. I felt that God was going to get us on the trail after all.

One last feeble attempt!

The next morning was glorious. The sun was bright and had started drying out the damp ground. I was anxious to get going and so were the other believers. We all met together next to Bob's house and decided to leave. A whoop went up from the young men who had become my personal entourage.

There were six teenagers who always hung around me watching my every move. We had enjoyed foot races, soccer, archery tournaments, and canoeing. Actually the canoeing thing was more like my getting into their long, narrow, hollowed-out logs and trying to stand up like all the other men did. Bob could do it. Many were the times Jungle Bob came and patiently showed me just how easy it really was. I would try my best to paddle, but without fail I would lose my balance and end up tumbling into the muddy river. Boy did they howl hysterically! It was as if they never grew tired of seeing me wobble around until disaster struck. Okay, so I had to paddle a canoe kneeling like the women. It was alright though, because I won lots of fruit from them in our archery contests! (see back cover photo)

"a Bisorio canoe"

So when the shout went out through the village that we were going to leave, everyone went crazy with excitement. People came out of their huts and women with babies clinging to them talked animatedly. I was a little confused about the order of everything, so I simply followed the young men down the trail through the village to the river below.

All of a sudden, we heard men shouting back in the village. The guys I was with turned around and began running the kilometer or so back to the house from which we had just come! What in the world could it be now?! I was a bit put out but decided to follow them and see what the uproar was all about.

When I came into view of Bob's house I noticed a group of people, all yelling and acting crazy, in a circle around Bob. As I jogged up to them, I discovered that some of the men had subdued a wild looking bushman who had apparently gone berserk. With a large branch he had bludgeoned the solar panels and radio we were taking up to Tsobu. It was the only time I had ever seen Bob angry. He called in the authorities and reported the man for attacking his guys who had been carrying the equipment. He then gathered up the two panels and radio that somehow still worked, wrapping them carefully.

We then all set off with determination in every step. This time when we arrived at the river, we crossed over!

3 Tsobu: The Hike

A great weight loss program!

It is interesting to me to hear of "hikes" that people take here in America. A woman once showed me pictures of her week-long hike in Arizona. The trails were well groomed and carefully marked so she and her companions couldn't get lost. Their backpacks were form fitted and adjusted scientifically to put just the right amount of weight onto the hips. They covered a total of twenty or so miles. The hikes I endured in the jungles and mountains of PNG were, well, very different!

When we set out, the men walked at a surprisingly fast gait. I thought it would be a cinch for me to keep up; I am significantly taller than they are and have longer legs. But I found it a challenge to keep pace with them. They were walking with bare feet and were not concerned about mud and water. I, on the other hand, was sporting my beautiful new $100 pair of Nike super hiking boots. At first, I worked hard not to get wet or slip off the slimy logs into the marsh on either side of the trail. That lasted for approximately five minutes! After a couple of "trips" into the hip-deep muck, I abandoned my pickiness! I began walking like a jungle man (except I didn't possess the balance, or the skill, or the strength). Okay, scratch that last statement — I began caring less about where I put my feet and just tried to keep pace with the rest of the men and the one lady with her baby. Yes, you heard that right — the young wife plus baby of my good friend Namolia had come along. Boy, would I grow in respect for her by the time this journey ended!

We slugged on through the swamp for a couple of hours. I gulped down my water and thirsted for more. My clothing was drenched with sweat, but I was thankful to God for helping me keep up. After all, I toted my Mathews solocam bow and a back pack with a couple cameras and some emergency rations for Bob and me. Bob was traveling light with nothing but a canteen and a walking stick — the wisdom of experience! I'm guessing Bob was close to 50 years old at the time, and I was very proud of him.

Everything was going well until I experienced a blowout in my left tire. I thought it was a lace or something and kept on a truckin'. But when the right one blew I had no choice. I stopped and inspected my expensive Nikes and to my horror discovered that they hadn't even lasted two hours!! I don't remember if it was the stitching or the glue that had come apart, but I dug into my backpack and quickly changed into the football cleats that I had brought along as spares. (Thanks Bob, you rock!)

I ran to catch up with the party. They knew that we had lost precious time with the crazy man incident. Darkness was coming.

We hiked through a big swamp, over a small mountain, and across a thorny jungle that first day. We had only traveled about 8 hours, but my body was pretty spent.

I washed in the river a bit, cleaning the places where kanda thorns had cut me up. Kanda is a whip-like vine that hangs down all over the jungle and is covered with thousands of thorns. They stick in your skin and sometimes break off, causing a great deal of discomfort. One time I was jumping across a small ravine and a limp hanging kanda vine snagged my arm whilst I was soaring through the air. The next thing I knew I was lying flat on my back wondering where all the pretty little stars floating around my head had come from!

So after washing my mud covered body, I headed back to the shore to inspect the dwelling where we would all somehow sleep that night. The structure was a raised floor with no walls around it, and leaves had been sown together and placed on top of the rafters as a roof. The floor was limbume, a type of bark that is flattened out and used to span the gap between the floor poles.

We were each given a sweet potato and a small piece of corn to eat. We then all just stretched out and went to sleep. I saw a large centipede crawling around, and the boys cut it up. I also noticed a large spider up in the roof, but since the Bisorios weren't worried about it I decided maybe I shouldn't be either.

Day Two

It seemed I had just fallen asleep when suddenly I looked up and the sun was peeking over the mountains upstream. I was lying there by myself and so got up quickly. Where was everyone? Looking around I spotted some people with Bob extracting our breakfast from the coals of last night's fire. I didn't want them thinking I was soft, but I couldn't ignore the soreness in my muscles. "Good," I consoled myself, "it just means that I'm getting stronger." Maybe you've also heard the saying: Pain is simply weakness leaving the body!

As soon as I got my stuff together, I was off. To my surprise one group of men had about an hour's head start. Bob and I were behind walking with the "slow ones." I was crushed. I wanted so badly to be considered a strong man.

We hiked for about six hours and finally came to a place where we could rest a bit. It was so beautiful. I was enjoying the ruggedness of all this, but I was going through two to four liters of water every hour! The guys looked at me and commented, *"Wede amabu tsiaka biamu, wede amabu tsaka dau"* (man, this is really something new I'm seeing). They stood staring at my face in amazement as the sweat poured off my chin in a rivulet the size of my little finger. *"Hone Davide* (white man David), if you would stop drinking all that water, you would stop leaking so badly." I explained that if I stopped drinking all that water, I would get heat stroke and die!

We moved on, starting up a very large mountain called Nobsiko (elevation 9455 feet). As I was hiking, I noticed that I was losing much of my hearing. This had never happened to me in America. But in the heat of the jungle, my hearing was changing and my head felt like it was going to explode from the pressure. I wondered how my heart could handle this duress because it beat so fast for so long. If you have ever wished to go on a diet that would purge your body of all fat and toxins, boy have I got a plan for you! We ate so little and exercised so much that I had no elimination for two weeks! My skin became so clean that it actually squeaked when I rubbed my arms together.

Whenever we came to a stream I rushed ahead and dove into it, holding my head under as long as I dared. It was a desperate attempt to cool my head down and it seemed to work quite well. I drank the water in the streams without filtering it because we were always on the go with no time for breaks.

We hiked all that second day until finally we came to a little structure in the tall grass. It was nothing more than some old sticks in the form of a lean-to that had some dry leaves still clinging to it. It wasn't exactly standing up, at least not all of it. We worked to prop it up a bit while Bob dug around in the gear for a 2 by 3 foot piece of plastic. He carefully tucked it up under the leaves directly over the place where our heads would rest. Good call, Bob. Someone cut a few banana leaves and spread them on the ground. We simply laid down on them and went to sleep. It was a tiny hut and we were all crammed in under it like sardines.

That night the sky dumped on us. The rain descended in sheets that drenched us all. At least the plastic in the roof over Bob and me kept the water from dripping onto our faces! If you hike for 12-14 hours of the day, you can sleep through pretty much anything!

The next morning we were all soaked. The rain had made little rivers all around us and some of our number had felt it all night long. A large spider was next to me when I opened my eyes. It obviously enjoyed the warmth of my body and the dryness of the leaf I was on. Glad it wasn't hungry!

Dage!

"Bob digging into 'dage'"

We typically had two meals per day whether we needed them or not — one in the morning before setting off and one after dark.

This morning was a special treat. You see, the tribe I was with had a culinary specialty — a substance they called "*dage.*"

In the Sepik jungle, strange looking pandanus trees grow. They look like enormous spiders crawling out of the ground. The roots grow up so high that one can walk right underneath them. The leaves are sharp fronds with barbs on the edges. Under the cluster of fronds grows a long tube covered with thousands of colored seeds. These seeds can be red, orange, or yellow when ripe and are slightly sweet tasting. The crispy white inside tastes like a rutabaga, but the people consider that pig food. They like to cut the two- to three-foot-long "fruit" into sections and then boil them in water. When the seeds become soft, the lower status tribespersons all gather around and chew up the seeds and then spit it out into a trough. The trough is made from the huge dished out stems of sago palm trees. The people spit this concoction into the trough and then stir it up. Chow Time! Everyone grabs a spoon or a stick and digs in.

Bob and I looked on with horror as we each got a spoon from our packs and gave thanks to our Creator for the food!

Is this making you want to become a missionary?

Since eating is such a big part of any culture, I will share with you a little game Bob and I played during the long hours of hiking that we so greatly enjoyed together. We "took each other out" to lunch or dinner or breakfast or supper or brunch or sometimes a dessert restaurant just to revel in our gluttony. Since this was all done from our imagination, our meals didn't cost us anything *and* we could eat all we wanted for hours and never gain a pound! As our bodies endured the countless hours of strenuous exercise, we sought to up the ante by making the other guy suffer. We tried in vain to outdo the other guy's fictitious feast! The funny thing is, what I craved the most was an apple from Washington State and a soda fountain Dr. Pepper with tons of ice in it. Poor Bob kept thinking about a steak dinner with an enormous piece of cherry cheesecake — or was that me?

Third day

I wish I could describe for you how intensely beautiful some of the places were that we came across in the jungle. Oh, how I longed to somehow take Gail to see these special little spots. We sometimes came to areas where waterfalls made natural wonderlands just like a water theme park. There were trees that were enormous. We trekked across areas from high up in the mountains that just took your breath away. We crossed over many mountains and even a vine bridge strung between two cliffs fifty feet above a raging river! At one point in our journey we found a wonderful place where the stream made all these little waterfalls as it worked its way down the rocky river bed. It was as if God had designed a place for weary hikers to sit in the cupped-out stone "chairs" and let the waters massage their aching muscles!

The third night we spent in a beautiful village called Amaleo situated at the top of a mountain ridge. The huts were built right along the steep mountainside with the crest of the hill leveled out for a town center. I sat on the porch of the hut where we slept and let my feet swing out into the open air. It was the first time since we started the hike that I wasn't all wet!! The hill dropped away sharply beneath me and I could look out over the valley and hillside below. It felt so good to let my legs dangle and to drink in the fresh cool mountain air. With much interest I watched a huge garden spider weave an impressive web between two tall banana trees just thirty feet away.

We stayed a couple of days at Amaleo so that Bob could meet with the Christian believers and review what they had learned. We also rested up a little in preparation for the last leg of the journey.

On to Tsobu

The last day of the journey was a grueling hike up a river. For many hours we were hopping from boulder to boulder. Then the trail got rough! There were times we climbed up nearly vertical faces, clinging to the roots of the peculiar trees that grew there. I had trouble hanging onto the roots, as I was carrying a compound bow in one hand. I wondered about Namolia's wife. She was carrying a baby, food, extras blankets, a pot or two, and I'm not really sure what else. When women are with a party of hikers they tend to be the ones carrying the biggest bundles!

As I walked along, carefully choosing each step along the edge of a cliff, the ground suddenly gave way beneath me. Falling straight down, I caught on some roots with my armpits. I somehow managed to *not* drop my bow! How does the woman holding the baby do it? I asked myself as I struggled to regain my footing. These Bisorio people are light and strong and they get around like mountain goats!

4 Tsobu: Twenty-six pass from death to life

*I once was lost but now am found,
Was blind but now I see.*
– <u>Amazing Grace</u>, John Newton

It was getting dark by the time we finally made it to the camp we called "Tsobu." This hamlet was maybe a mile or two from Denaya's village.

Tsobu was high up in the mountains, where it rained almost every night. It was a bit chilly up here, especially for the Christian Bisorios who normally lived just above sea level. These committed ones had no gardens and no real comforts here. The only reason they came was for the purpose of giving the gospel to these poor souls in Denaya's clutches.

We were shown the tiny hut that had been built for us. It was affectionately labeled "the pastor house." It was a special little place maybe eight feet long by eight feet wide and only 5 feet high. The door was so short that I often scraped the skin off the back of my neck upon entering the little room. When Bob and I stretched out our bed rolls, three or four other guys wanted to sleep in there with us. I don't know if they were afraid of the demon Denaya or just hoping that with more bodies it would be warmer inside. It was definitely cramped!

We had very little to eat while up there. We typically enjoyed a sweet potato for breakfast and two after dark for supper. I had saved some rice for Bob and myself so that we could supplement our feast. We certainly weren't living "high on the hog"!

One really fun thing we did every evening was play a game called "Assassin." About 30 of us would cram into a smoke filled hut. The game was conducted in the Bisorio language, which I was struggling to learn. This quickly became the highlight of the evening. The people always wanted "just one more game." One man gets the cards and orders the game. He is the narrator and always has his eyes open. Everyone else who wants to play assumes an identity based on the card they're given. There are two assassins, one policeman, a judge, a doctor and the rest are regular civilians. After everyone closes their eyes, the two assassins point to one person they want to take out. After the victim is selected, the assassins close their eyes and the narrator gives the doctor a chance to heal one person. The policeman is then given a chance to send one person to jail. After that all open their eyes and the narrator exclaims, "A murder has been committed." Everyone tries hard to figure out who the assassins are and then votes out one person they suspect. The assassins try desperately to put the blame on someone else to keep from getting caught. You can't imagine what chaos ensued when Bob and I both became assassins in the same game. Here the two missionaries are taking out the civilians like crazy and no one can doubt a word we say! But the absolute worst was when I was an assassin and Bob was a regular guy. We both did some pretty fancy talking and the people were so confused they finally voted Bob out! I guess you'd have to have been there!

Pig hunt

I usually got up before light and went out in an attempt to shoot a certain huge pig. Evidently some villager's very large male pig had gone feral. This brute had gathered for himself a group of female pigs and decided that was a much better arrangement than being in the confines of a wooden shelter! This pig, we'll call him "the beast," had been very naughty and had broken through a fence

Miracles in the Jungle

into someone's garden. He and his hungry harem had devastated much of the gardens in the area. So the people tried to kill and eat "the beast."

It would probably be a good time for me to point out a couple of interesting facts regarding male pigs, called boars. They love to eat, and can grow very large. I have seen photos of boars weighing nearly 1000 pounds! They fight with tusks that grow out of the sides of their mouths. They use these sharp tusks to hook their opponent. God designed a thick cartilage plate on both sides of their ribcage to shield the vital organs from an opponent's tusks.

If a man shot a bamboo arrow into the pig's chest, it would simply turn on the hapless hunter and attempt to kill him! According to the men of the place, this pig had "eaten" three men who had decided to hunt it. I was excited! I wanted to hunt this pig and demonstrate the power of the Matthews solo cam bow. The men thought this funny. They started making jokes about what the pig would do to me. Would you care to hear one of their "jokes"?

Yalamai (a tribal guy of epic fame to these people) said, "That pig will smell you, white man, and turn to look at you." The group of onlookers snickered with glee. "He will charge you and you will turn to run away." More laughter. "Then he will strike you with his mouth and knock you to the ground." Guys were starting to clutch their sides and some at this point were rolling on the earth. "Then he will rake you with his tusks from side to side." By now everyone had tears streaming from their eyes. "AND THEN THE BLOOD WILL COME SHOOTING OUT!" The people were now all on the ground laughing so hard that they had lost control. I just stood there amazed at what *ever* kind of humor this could be. They all stared at me to see what I would say to this.

"*Wede haila, plise wede haila*" (I would really really like that). It was kind of lame, but it was the only thing I could think of. They all erupted in a renewed burst of uncontrolled mirth. Inside I wanted to get that pig at all cost.

The only man willing to guide me on my initial hunt was a true bush man from Tsobu named Sebi. He got me up at about 3 a.m. We quickly walked through the village and up the mountain to the south. The first obstacle we came to was a narrow log about thirty

Miracles in the Jungle

feet long, used to traverse a shallow ravine. Sebi skillfully ran along it as if it was a super highway. I tried to balance but, do you recall my steadiness with the canoe? About half way across I started wobbling. I thought that I had recovered but my foot slipped and I fell right onto my ribcage. It knocked the wind out of me. I then bounced off the log and fell into a garden below. Landing on my back, I barely missed a pointed stake sticking out of the ground. It pierced through my shirt scraping my armpit. Talk about a close call!

But there was no time to dwell on my close shave with death. Sebi was sizzling up the trail and I didn't dare get left behind. After about an hour, we arrived at the big garden. We climbed up and onto a dead tree where we could see much of the garden and waited. Sebi rolled up some tobacco and started to smoke. I asked him if he was going to reveal our presence with the scent of tobacco, but he brushed his hand to the side and declared that this pig fears nothing! I was glad to hear that, because I really wanted to stick "the beast" with one of my expensive expandable broad heads!

Soon we heard the sound of pigs in the underbrush near the garden fence only 50 yards away. My heart started beating a bit quicker and I got an arrow ready on the string. Suddenly, the pigs stopped their approach and then after a few moments left. Sebi looked at me with a puzzled expression on his face. He wanted to go back.

As we returned to Tsobu, I asked him to teach me how to walk fast through the slippery sections — especially going downhill. He showed me how to run down steep places using little flat spots to check your speed a bit. With some practice I learned this technique. Many times since then it served me well as I traveled with other New Guinea natives. Many fellow hikers have been impressed by this Sepik *kanaka's* (wild bush man's) way of descending the mountains!

The next day no one was willing to take me hunting. It was as if the people were wondering why "the beast" that feared no one would not come into the garden while I was there. I hunted that pig alone every day following, determined to kill it, but I never got a single shot at it. I wondered if the demon Denaya had anything to do with keeping the pigs away. Or was it simply the fact that my scent was different from the locals? I never found out. What I did know is that day by day Bob and I were becoming lighter, and I was becoming a more fit individual, able to hike around the mountains with greater skill and dexterity.

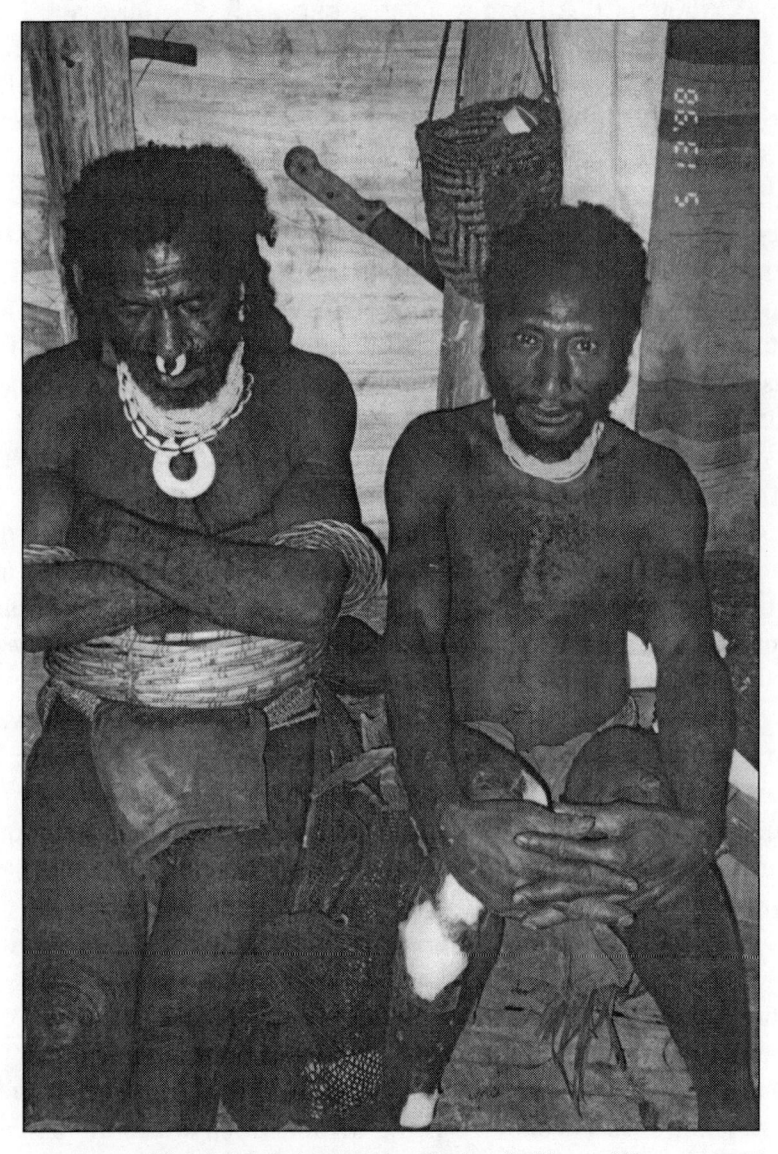

"Sebi (right) - a new Tsobu believer!"

The table and benches

One thing I quickly grew weary of up on that soggy mountaintop was squatting in the mud or sitting on a wet log. I never felt rested. We here in the lap of American luxury have so much comfort around us at all times. We bathe or shower in a temperature controlled environment. We sit down for hours at a time in very comfortable chairs and eat at tables ergonomically correct to fit our anatomy. In the jungle you just squat or perhaps sit on a rotting tree trunk! It rained a great deal on top of that mountain and it chilled me when I wasn't working. So I decided to do something about it.

The thing that got me thinking was seeing a man skillfully split a tree right down the middle and make boards out of it. I asked him if I could try and found out that with a little practice I too could make boards from a log with an axe!

The six young men that were constantly watching my every move (when I wasn't hunting for food — we were vegetarians due to my lack of success!) joined me with much enthusiasm. We drove stakes into the clay soil near a large fire pit and built a large sturdy table. When that was finished you couldn't keep the guys off of it! They all fought over who got to lay on it and set their bags on it. The women eyed it enviously, wishing to use it for their needs.

I began working on benches around the fire when a "big man" (an older man with some importance in the societal structure) came and started complaining about the work we were doing.

"Our ancestors never did anything like this!" He shouted with a very angry look on his face. "You can't come here and make us live like you white men." He banged a stick onto the top of the table for emphasis. All eyes turned to see my response.

"It's okay," I assured Hamiagu (the angry man), "I am not as strong as you people are. It hurts my knee joints to be sitting on them all the time. I will just use this for myself while I'm here, and when I leave you can tear them all down and burn the wood."

Hamiagu turned his back and stomped off a little way, then spun around and watched as we continued our work.

Now I am no psychologist by any stretch of the imagination, but I knew that others would want to use anything that I made for myself. So in constructing the benches, I started with those on the far side of the fire pit across from where I eventually wanted to position my own personage! I finished the first bench along the southern side of the pit and lost approximately five helpers (they were sitting there with their feet propped up making sure the bench wasn't going anywhere). I finished the west side bench and a few more placed their bags on the table and then sat down to try out this crazy new contraption. The last bench I purposely made extra long as I figured guys would want to sit with me. On one end I made it jumbo-size to fit me — and I even splurged and installed a back rest so I could put my arms up. I made sure that a large stone was in front of this area so that the fire could heat the stone and warm my feet! Nice! When one's feet are constantly wet, it is wonderful to get them dry and warm.

Upon finishing, I went to put the axe and machete inside the "pastor house." It had started to drizzle a bit. When I turned around I was shocked! There sat Hamiagu in MY seat. He had his feet up on the stone and his arms outstretched on the back rest! Instead of being angry with him, I thought "This man too is made in the image of God. We as humans are not evolved animals and as such are not made to live in the mud like them."

We all had a new experience that evening as we gathered around the table and benches and warmed ourselves. Who doesn't enjoy a good campfire experience?! The only thing missing was the s'mores!

Teaching the Word of God - the Eternal Reward

While we constructed the "church" building where the Bible would be taught twice daily, messengers were sent out to invite people to come to our little mountain top village to hear God's Talk.

Some had no interest in coming. One man who lived in a cave with his two daughters told the messenger, "Do you see the stone walls of this cave quaking? My heart is like these stones; it does not fear your God."

As I have reflected on this cave man over the years, I believe that his attitude and reasoning is very similar to men and women we call "scientists" who believe in humanism and the gospel of evolution.

They too have hard hearts and do not fear God, even though they also will someday stand before Him and be judged by His righteous standard.

Others came and sat day-in and day-out hearing the whole Bible taught from the creation account to Christ's death, burial and resurrection. (I believe it took approximately six months.) Twenty-six people decided that they wanted to "live inside the fence of Jesus Christ." Praise the Lord! Although very few here on this earth even knew of these new Tsobu believers, the angels in heaven rejoiced. Jesus left the ninety-nine to find the one, and in a similar way, this one last village was worth it all for eternity!

5 Tsobu: Back Home

A dry leaf does not laugh when his neighbor falls.
– Chinese proverb

I did not stay in Tsobu past the first few weeks. I was only with Bob for about a month. One day I heard on the radio schedule that a special flight was coming to the Bisorio airstrip. I was not needed any longer and Bob asked if I wanted to go back home. I really missed Gail and the boys and decided I wanted to try to get back in time to catch the flight. It had taken us four days of hard hiking (plus two days of rest at Amaleo) to come up to Tsobu - and I only had two days to make it back if I wanted to get on that plane!

I asked Ramon, a friend from the village of Amaleo whom I'd grown to respect, if he would guide me back. He agreed to get me as far as Amaleo but no further. From there on I would have to rely on Lewaybe.

Let me tell you about Lewaybe. He was a laid-back man who had lived through a bout of cerebral malaria. This form of malaria kills many people, and for those who do survive, it can cause them to be retarded for the rest of their lives. Even though Lewaybe was a bit slow, he had a heart for the things of the Lord. One morning when I was out hunting, Bob heard him wake up and turn over onto his stomach. He prayed, "Lord, we are up here in this cold place. We have little food and are really hungry. We don't have our family here, but have only come because You told us to. So please cause this garden to grow that You are planting through us." I believe that the gist of his simple prayer was "God, it is really hard for us to be here. It's miserable and a huge sacrifice on our part. Don't let it be for nothing!"

I liked Lewaybe, he was a nice, patient man. But he was not exactly what you would consider "light of foot" — if you know what I mean. I was worried that he would not be able to go very fast and that he would keep me from getting to the plane in time. When I first came to PNG I was told by some that the tribal people were "masters of the jungle" and that they were so strong and swift they could beat any white man in hiking. Well, some certainly are brilliant and some very gifted in hiking through the jungle... but let's be truthful, some folks just never get out of first gear all their lives, regardless of the amount of melanin their skin contains!

A bunch of men from Amaleo came to see Ramon. I overheard their conversation and this is what they said:

"Oh Ramon, you are in for some pain. That white guy will slow you down. White men have stupid feet and you will have to pick him up all the time. We'll speed on back to Amaleo and be sitting up on our porches watching for you guys to arrive in the darkness with rain pouring down on your heads."

They laughed a great deal, not knowing that I could now understand much of what they were saying!

Ramon finally turned and walked toward me. "Don't worry Ramon, I won't slow you down. Just help me a little bit with some of the weight in my pack and we will go like *kanakas* (wild jungle men)!"

A smile came over his face as he started taking a couple of items out of my pack.

I said good bye to Bob and we were off!

After an hour or two we had to wait for Lewaybe. After two more hours we had to wait almost 45 minutes for him to catch up! Finally Ramon assured me, "Lewaybe is a man of this place, he won't get lost. Let's beat those other guys who were laughing at you back to Amaleo."

Game on! We tore up the boulder-strewn river's edge like wild men. Every hill and tough spot in the trail barely slowed us down at all. I had lost almost 25 pounds and I felt like I could go a hundred miles! We made it back to Amaleo in record time! We washed in the river at the foot of the mountain and then hiked back up to the village on top.

"Amaleo"

We ate a nice meal and just rested. A couple hours later we watched as dark clouds rolled in. It was going to rain and with a vengeance! The three men still had not arrived and there was no sign of Lewaybe. I was beginning to worry. An hour later the sky exploded in a torrent of rainfall. I was really concerned about Lewaybe. Was he alright? What could he do in this deluge? The next day he was to be my one and only guide back to Bisorio!

Finally we saw the three men walking briskly in the rain along the slippery mountainside trail. They were holding banana leaves over their heads to keep the rain off, but it wasn't working very well! The look in their eyes, when they caught sight of me sitting on the porch above the trail with my legs dangling over, was priceless! I really should have had a camera (with night vision)! Everything those guys had said about me was happening to them. I smiled warmly to them, "Oh good, you three come, ah?"

I prayed for Lewaybe, that our Father would guide him in. Then I set my alarm for 4:30 a.m.

Hands down, the most severe storm that I had ever experienced raged all that night. Land slides thundered down the slopes around us. Lightning ripped across the sky as if a comet had struck the earth. The thunder was deafening, keeping us from sleeping soundly. Would this hut clinging tenuously to the side of the mountain hold? If my faith in the power of God hadn't been so strong, I would have moved to some other place that very night! "...In Your book they all were written, the days fashioned for me, when as yet there were none of them." — the words from the book of Psalms gave me comfort. I listened as the sides of mountains gave way, descending to the river below. Huge trees that had stood for a hundred years crashed down. Some sounded like they were just outside our little hut!

Amaleo to Bisorio

The next morning, I woke up a very reluctant Lewaybe. We grabbed a sweet potato and hit the trail. I couldn't believe my eyes. The trail was devastated only fifty yards from where we started. We had three days of hiking to squeeze into one, and we were spending up to 5 minutes negotiating each of the many huge trees that littered the mountainside. All of this from just one storm the night before.

It also cost us precious energy and strength, and for me, injury! You see, some of these enormous trees fallen across the trail were 10 feet high and some were sloping steeply downhill. When I tried to climb over them, I often slipped and fell to the ground. This was very entertaining to Lewaybe, but for me, very painful! The trunks were wet and my football cleats would not hold. Lewaybe was bare footed and doing just fine. I had a bow and arrow in one hand and a heavy pack on my back. He had both hands free with just a small bag strung around his shoulder.

We finally made it past the land slides and carnage, but what should have taken us 20 -30 minutes had taken us almost two hours! I had a little pow-wow with my hiking buddy! "I **have** to make it back to Bisorio by tonight. We are going too slow right now and we must start walking stronger." He smiled that crooked smile that made him look so funny, but it wasn't funny now!

We crossed the vine bridge and the river beneath us was a boiling torrent. I prayed that the bridge would hold!

Then came the hike up Nobsiko mountain. I put my heart into the climb and soon was out of sight of my partner. I stopped and shouted back for him to hurry up! He grunted and told me to just go on. So I did. I decided to get to the top and then rest while I waited for him. I reached the top and realized two things: one, when you stop, the mosquitoes swarm you; and two, I wasn't in need of a rest! So I hiked on. The trail was so nice, I decided to start jogging. Man, I felt great. I was probably in the best shape of my life. I ran on and on, feeling strong, the forest floor flying by.

Then a wonderful idea came to me. I remembered the place where a special stream had carved out perfect sitting pools. If I could just find that place in the trail, I could sit and soak in the soothing waters cascading all around me as I waited for Lewaybe to catch up!

I was so pumped about being able to relax and cool off that I kind of lost track of where I was. I slowed to a walk in an attempt to bring to mind something of the area in which I now found myself. I didn't recognize any of this! I had been running down the mountain thinking that the stream should be just ahead, but now nothing looked familiar to me. I decided to turn around and run back up the hill that I'd just descended. Then I worked my way down to a stream that I could hear at the bottom of a ravine in order to gain my bearings. Bad move! It was so dense and steep that I used significant amounts of energy going down and much more coming back up. I then retraced my steps and wondered if I had gone down a wrong trail. I panicked a little and started yelling for Lewaybe. No reply.

I thought perhaps Lewaybe might have passed by during my excursion down into the ravine, so I made for the top of the ridge. Frantically, I yelled and yelled. Now I had wasted over an hour in this foolishness, and I was starting to become weary and very hungry. I ran down the trail a mile or so only to retrace my steps again! I was scared and started yelling like crazy for him.

I lost my voice just as Lewaybe came into view. Now my strength was gone. And to my horror, he suddenly decided we were in trouble and started moving with some passion in his stride. I could scarcely believe my eyes when we hiked to the bottom of the hill that I had gone up and down no fewer than four times and found that the waterfall wonder park I had sought was only fifty yards further through the dense spot in the trees!

I now struggled desperately to keep up with Lewaybe. My legs kept cramping up. I couldn't yell to him because my voice was hoarse. Traveling in and out of swampy areas, I kept getting lost and sometimes got stuck in the soft, stinking muck. My energy was wasted, my legs would not behave, and my desperate calls to him were useless as my throat just emitted a raspy sound.

After an hour we finally came out at the foot of the mountain where a small structure offered us a rest. I was REALLY in bad shape. I asked Lewaybe to find me some sugarcane and some ginger root. I had saved one can of chili for my trek back and offered to share it with him. He said he didn't want any. That was a miracle! He normally loved any kind of new food. He gave me the sugar cane and ginger and I ate the can of chili. Then we set off.

The transformation was remarkable. God had given my body the ability to absorb enough salts and sugars to get me back in the game again. But we had a day and a half's worth of hiking still to do in the six hours left before the darkness of night would fall! The bad thing was, we had to cross a very swollen river due to the previous night's rainfall.

There is so much irony in life. At first I kept falling down and hurting myself because of my shoes. Lewaybe had laughed at me mercilessly. Now on the muddy lowlands, my cleats were doing their job, hooking up very well, and it was Lewaybe who was constantly slipping and falling down.

We hiked along the river, crossing it often. The water level was high and it kept sweeping my little traveling buddy away! I don't think Lewaybe could swim. There was one time the water took him and he flopped around comically. I gave chase, grabbed the poor guy, and hauled him in to more shallow waters. From then on, I just stayed with "Shorty" and held his hand every time we made a

Miracles in the Jungle

crossing. He kind of floundered around at the end of my arm, his feet touching nothing. I thought it humorous but didn't so much as crack a smile! We were in this thing together; we needed each other.

We hiked with all our might, mile after mile, making good time in spite of the poor conditions. Another ironic thing happened. On our way up to Tsobu, we couldn't find any game to shoot along the way. But now, Lewaybe and I were passing up all kinds of critters that I could easily have "harvested" with my bow!

The pack was rubbing my back raw and I was a bloody mess from the kanda vines and thorns we plowed through. We had to make it over the last mountain before darkness closed in. When the sun goes down in the jungle, it becomes incredibly dark due to the dense foliage and muddy forest floor.

We had barely made it up one side of the last mountain when darkness overtook us. I had a Mini Maglite and turned it on. We worked our way carefully down the mountain and into the swamp. At times I had to swim across croc-infested ponds with the bow in one hand and the flashlight in my teeth. **I know** God protected us during this stage!! Finally my little flashlight bulb burned out and now we were stuck! We were so close. We worked our way to the bank of the Krosmeri River (Angry Woman River) that separated us from the village up on the other side.

In a hoarse voice, I asked Lewaybe to signal the village to send someone out to come get us. He did, but I'll never know how. About 45 minutes later we were in a canoe, crossing a very swollen and fast-flowing river. I relaxed for the first time since our "lunch break."

On the other side, there remained one last mile that separated me from the house where a missionary named Greg would provide me with some food, a shower, and a bed.

That last mile was flat, most of it being the mowed airstrip, but my legs weren't working so well. The cramping had returned and every step was a struggle.

When I got to Greg's house he invited me in and set some dinner before me. I first needed to get the clothes I was wearing off, so I could attend to my wounds. When I removed my shirt, I discovered that the pack had worn a hole in my back near my hip. My underwear had worn the skin raw around my legs. Lots and lots of owies for Gail to nurse — I couldn't wait!

Even though the water stung like crazy, it never felt so good to take a shower. I was so thankful to be back in "civilization"!

Greg's meal was superb — a secret recipe that his wife had created called "taco soup." Think of the best soup you've ever had, times it by three, and you might know how good it tasted!

HOME!

The next day, I flew back to my little family in Maprik. They were to rendezvous with us at the airstrip in Hayfield. I had it all planned out — I would hug and kiss my wife first and then hold my two little boys. However, when I arrived and stepped out of the Cessna 206, my friend's gregarious son Levi came running up and threw his arms around me. "Uncle Davie," he squealed with delight, "I really missed you!" I hugged him back and then carried him over to where my wife and boys, and his dad, were waiting.

Baby Seth didn't know what to think. I had lost so much weight that he didn't recognize me, plus I'd grown a beard. Jonny just wanted to show me the new bug that he'd carefully brought along. And Gail just held me tight not saying anything at all. I wept a bit, so thankful to be back with my precious family.

I promised myself that from then on I would keep the weight off and eat only things that were good for me. But when we got to our little apartment, Gail presented a beautiful cherry cheesecake that she had made just for me. I ate only one piece — if half the pie can be considered one piece! I saved the other piece for the next day. I didn't want anyone thinking I didn't possess any will power, and I didn't want to hurt my wife's feelings!

Some people might feel that tribal people are better off left alone. But everyone needs an opportunity to learn of their Creator and to understand how much He wants them to be with Him. Is that really such a horrible message? A message of life from death? Of light instead of darkness? May we never take our own salvation for granted and may it be our aim to make His Name known in all the world!

6 Gail's Trial

"For I consider that the sufferings of this present time are not worthy to be compared with the glory which shall be revealed in us." Romans 8:18

"**P**ray for me, Dave, I'm having some pain in my abdomen." There was something in her voice that caused me great concern.

I was far away out in a bush location called Nakwi and had been talking with the two missionary families there about the possibility of joining them in their work. My wife had checked up on me at 7 p.m., the scheduled radio time when all the missionaries reported in from their various locations. It was now midnight. That evening the two families and I had been discussing our visions, strategies, and philosophies, but I couldn't keep from thinking of Gail. Finally I asked them to pray with me for my wife. We then said good night and I went to my room to sleep.

I awoke suddenly to the sound of a Cessna 206 circling over the jungle house. It was first light and too early for planes to be flying under normal circumstances. I knew immediately something was wrong. I threw on my clothes, grabbed my pack, and headed out in haste. Dianne offered me some breakfast but I declined. Tim was on the radio with the pilot. "Gail's sick, and Bret has come here to fly you out — he'll meet you at the Iteri airstrip."

I asked for two young men to guide me through the jungle to the airstrip at Iteri. They offered to carry the pack. I told them, "I'll

Miracles in the Jungle

carry the pack; we need to run like strong men and not slow down." They looked puzzled but then, seeing me start to run in the direction of Iteri, took off as well.

It was starting to rain.

As I ran I began to recall all the times that I had complained about my wife. God had blessed me with a very special woman and yet I had managed to find some things for which I didn't care. I had, in fact, been unthankful. The guilt of my ingratitude rained down hard on me, just as the rain outside my mind was now doing. I mean to tell you, it was a mini deluge! I wondered if the plane would be able to take off in this rain.

The jungle is an interesting place — you either love it or hate it. It can be a friend at times, where you can be so alone and feel so close to God. And at other times it is a stinking, filthy, muddy nightmare where the noise of the katydids seems deafening. This morning, the light was dim under the canopy of growth and it was muddy and slippery.

I had always been a good runner and had never allowed my body to get too far out of shape. It was always my desire to be able to get out and trek with the natives through the jungle. Often I would hear comments about white people being weak and unable to go very far. Native guys would say to me, "The place is about three days of hard walking from here, but one of us could do it in a day." It had seemed that, with a proper level of motivation, I too could "do it in a day." And now, oddly enough, I was feeling just a tinge of pride as the two young men "running nothing" (running without carrying anything) had difficulty in keeping up with me.

It is best to point out here that most of the jungle folk that I have had the pleasure of hiking with do not run. Once in a while you may see a young man run, but on long hikes they typically walk with a steady gait. We were running and, as I mentioned, they were struggling to keep up.

I was really motivated to get to that plane. Unfortunately, the villages of Nakwi and Iteri were not on friendly terms at that time, so the trail linking the two was very rough and indistinct. It was sometimes difficult to know which way to go. The actual distance separating the two may have been as little as three miles as the crow flies, but the trail length back then was perhaps five miles. It took 90 minutes for someone walking briskly to complete the trek.

It seems that pride had bitten me and so the Lord graciously gave me a loving reminder to be humble! As I sped along the muddy trail in the driving rain, I came upon a large log. Without a second's hesitation, I decided to jump over it. My foot slipped and my shin slammed into the trunk. Pain shot through my shin like lava burning down the leg. Wiping the mud and blood away, I got a better look — it wasn't broken although it felt that way! The two guys had not caught up with me yet, so I pushed on, feeling very humbled. "God, please forgive my foolish pride," I mumbled as I jogged on.

And now what of this other form of pride in my ungratefulness toward my wife? It was as if in that moment God asked me, "Do you want her?" or "Do you think you can do better?" I didn't hesitate, "No, God, don't let her die. I'm so sorry. Don't let her die." With each pounding, throbbing pain shooting through my leg, I cried out to God.

Things started looking a little more familiar, and I started running faster. Forty-five minutes of extreme emotion and pain, and I was now almost to Iteri.

When I came out onto the expanse of green, I looked and saw the plane halfway up the 900-yard grass airstrip. On reaching it, I noticed the pilot looked very concerned. You see, due to the nature of this emergency, he had bent the rules a bit by leaving before sunup to fly down here to the Sepik region. But now, after landing, the clouds had simply closed in like giant hands holding the plane down. Bret looked at me and said, "I'm so sorry, Dave, we can't go until the clouds clear up."

I pointed straight ahead with my finger and shouted "God, make a hole in the clouds!"

He did!

Bret didn't miss a beat. He throttled the plane up and we shot forward toward that small opening above the end of the runway. The clouds actually closed back together after we passed through them; I know, because I was watching.

"Iteri airstrip"

I was flown the 100 miles or so to an airstrip where we would rendezvous with the larger mission plane. During that time I thought back to the treacherous jungle path where I had slipped and almost broken my leg. It was really hurting now that I had time to relax. I also thought of how I had so desperately prayed to God for my wife and how I had repented of my selfish thoughts. I really did need her, although I'd been ungrateful at times when she had not given me what I wanted. Now I just wanted her to live.

When Bret and I touched down in Hayfield, the doctor, Gail, and the boys hadn't arrived yet. A group of national people were there, and they approached this lone white man who had such a worried look on his face.

Their leader asked with concern, *"Gut de masta, yu orait o nogat? Fes bilong yu i no hamamas tumas."* (Good day, sir, are you alright? Your face is not very happy)

I told him that I'd just come from the jungle, that my wife was bleeding to death, and I was waiting for her to arrive so that we could go to a hospital.

"She will not die," this smiling Christian man told me confidently. "We will pray to Father God." They all huddled around and we joined hands, praying fervently to our Father God in the name of His only begotten Son Jesus.

The burden instantly left my shoulders, and the group of forty or so national Christians walked away, singing as they went.

Moments later the Land Rover arrived with Gail atop a stack of cheap foam mattresses. We smiled when we saw each other. There is a cost in serving Christ that some will never have the privilege to pay. It may be a reputation or a dream job or some financial sacrifice. But all believers in Christ who choose to truly live for Him will suffer.

Gail's story

We lived on a small missionary base about 70 miles by road from the beautiful coastal town of Wewak. We were only two miles outside a very small town called Maprik, but jungle grew all around us. The base had a large workshop, two resident missionary homes, and five orientation apartments. It was December 1998, and we had been in PNG almost one year.

For a few weeks I'd been having some abdominal pain often accompanied with slight dizziness. Around midnight on December 10, I awoke and went to the bathroom, and it was then that I had the most excruciating pain. I was in such distress and so weak that I barely got back to the bed. I then tried to take a quick sip of water but fainted. When I later awoke, all wet from the spilled water, I sensed that I was dying. I pled with the Lord to spare my life. Later we found out that this was an ectopic or tubal pregnancy. I was bleeding internally and had only about four hours to live unless I could get to a hospital.

No one was around to hear my weak cries for help. Dave was gone, our neighbors upstairs were gone, and when my three year old son awoke he wasn't able to unlock the front door to go get someone. I kept trying to call out, but I realized no one lived close enough, plus most everyone had noisy fans blowing on them anyway in this kind of humidity.

The first miracle was that on that very night a national man was staying in the dormitory above the workshop. These dorm rooms were hardly ever used except during the annual conference. He was there just that one night and he was the one who heard me. He went to alert another missionary and then, after about two or three hours, I had help at my side.

One of the missionary orientees happened to be a nurse and, again, to me this was not just coincidence. God had her there! After checking my pulse and having trouble finding it, she quietly but urgently expressed to the others a need for an IV. She had none, and our base had none, but in town there was a small Catholic compound. Our only hope was that they might have one.

A missionary named Mike drove his Land Rover pickup to the compound in town. On reaching the locked gate, he found there was no security man to open it up. No one responded to his calls and honking. The fence around the property was too high for Mike to climb, but it seems the Lord had prepared a solution. Mike had considered unloading a 55-gallon drum off his Land Rover the day before, but for some reason felt he should just leave it. It was that drum that gave him the added height he needed to get over the security wire! The supplies were available and given to him, and soon Rachel the nurse (after many brave attempts) had an IV in my arm.

It was still looking very critical and the mission doctor had been called. Plans were to fly him up to our base as soon as it was light enough and then to medevac me out to either a PNG hospital or to Cairns, Australia. He arrived at my bedside around 6:30 a.m. and quickly checked things over. He then directed that I be put on the bed of that same Land Rover to make the 15-minute extremely bumpy journey down to Hayfield where the mission's Twin Otter plane waited.

*This was certainly more than four hours after my fallopian tube had ruptured, and according to the medical experts I should **not** have been alive. I believe God clotted the rupture with His own careful hand and kept me from bleeding to death. He is able!*

Dave was waiting for me at Hayfield, having flown in from Iteri. The larger plane took us all to a PNG hospital in Goroka. They gave me an ultrasound but it was inconclusive. So we continued on to the capital city of Port Moresby for clearance to leave the country, and then we finally flew to Cairns, Australia. This took all day, and what I remember is a lot of pain and nausea in very uncomfortable heat, but there was an overriding peace through it all.

When I was finally rolled into surgery in Cairns, the smiling Aussie doctor really didn't believe our mission doctor's diagnosis of an ectopic pregnancy. But afterward, he commented that there must be a God because he realized, as did we, that this was truly a miracle. To God be the glory!

The cost of this emergency was very large. More than $26,000 in bills accumulated. Nevertheless, the hundreds of dear Christians praying for us gave enough to cover the bills to a tee! It is so amazing and wonderful that when we have greater need, our Father gives us more than usual. And conversely, when the need is diminished, our income is lessened.

"...Give me neither poverty nor riches— Feed me with the food allotted to me; Lest I be full and deny You, and say, 'Who is the LORD?' Or lest I be poor and steal, and profane the name of my God." (Proverbs 30:8, 9)

My time of healing was very rapid. The 60 % of blood I'd lost was miraculously and quickly re-supplied by the Great Physician. It was much faster than the doctor predicted; he said that it would be at least six weeks before my body could make up for what I'd lost and that I'd be pretty weak. But at the beginning of the second week, we as a family were out shopping at the mall, enjoying a few luxuries of the first world!

We went to see the new movie "Prince of Egypt" and I was impressed with its ending. Having seen God's mighty hand of judgment through the plagues in Egypt, and having crossed the Red Sea on dry land and then looking back to see their enemies drowned in that same sea, the Israelites were now walking on toward the Promised Land. But what was their response in the upcoming hard times and testings? Unbelief and complaining — even after such tremendous miracles! I wondered if that is what I do at times (the answer is yes) and if I too would forget God's great work in saving my life there in the jungles of New Guinea. May God help us to be always in awe of everything that He has done, is doing, and will do for us His children!

7 Schultze

"Let the big dogs eat!" – author presumed dead

Being a missionary means lots and lots of work! One of the important jobs on the field is "supply buyer." This person purchases needed items in town and send them out to the other missionaries in bush locations. These supplies include things like rice, sugar, flour, powdered milk, canned food, soda pop, beef crackers, food seasonings, toiletries, batteries, bush knives, axes, tools, and medicines. The supply buyer is responsible for getting all requested items purchased, packed up, and weighed. Then these parcels are loaded onto the mission plane and the pilot flies them into the various tribal locations.

A year after we arrived in Papua New Guinea, there was a lack of help in the Sepik Region's supply role. The regional committee asked us to fill that need. So we moved to Wewak, a beautiful town on the northeastern coast of PNG.

Being there, however, meant living inside a fenced base. When you live in a third world country, there are many people who find it easier to "pinch" possessions at night while the missionaries sleep rather than to work for those same things. "Besides," they reason, "all white people are rich and they certainly won't be hurt too badly if we take some of their things." So the need for security always exists when you live on a base in town.

"Ocean view from Wewak base"

Some say "a dog is man's best friend." That's probably because the guy who started that wonderful little quote didn't live in a third world country surrounded by thieves — sorry, surrounded by opportunists! To a missionary, a good dog is more like a man's guardian

Miracles in the Jungle

angel! Most missionaries use German Shepherds as they are intelligent, loyal, tough, and basically the best dogs in the whole world. (just my humble unbiased opinion, of course) They can be **very** helpful in keeping people honest!

Schultze was just such a dog. Tipping the scales at 120 pounds, he was the perfect size for the task at hand. Schultze's master was a pilot with another mission who needed someone to care for him since this man was leaving for the States. I told him we would be grateful for the chance to have a guard dog and happy to look after his beautiful beast of a dog!

But there was a problem — he stunk! Poor old Schultze hadn't had a tubby in months. Well, I thought, what better way for us to bond? You know, a couple of buddies getting to know each other over a bubble bath!

So I secured a friend's small wading pool and proceeded to fill it up with water, being careful to insert copious amounts of dish detergent. Whistling merrily, I then went in search of my great, big, brand new, stinky doggy.

In hindsight, I suppose Schultze was probably a bit shell shocked from losing his life long friend. At the time, I wasn't exactly sensitive to his loss and I simply took hold of him with a good grasp. He stubbornly followed, resisting all the way, not seeming to long for that clean, fresh, fragrant feeling that I was so eager to give him!

So taking a firm grip on said dog, I forced him into the water — and he jumped out. I assisted him in again — he jumped out! I shoved him forcefully, wanting to show him that I was his new master and that he *was* going to be dunked into the water! He exploded violently and bit my hand! **It was on!**

My wife doesn't have an official degree in psychology, but she definitely could teach an informative class on "A" type personalities. I've tried in vain to explain to her that "A" stands for affectionate, able, amorous, articulate, amusing, a blessing, a really nice and kind person, a really good husband, and a humble sort of guy. But she never seems to buy it. In her mind I'm abrasive, aggressive, adventuresome, ambitious, annoying, abnormal, absurd, and sometimes a nerd!

Miracles in the Jungle

In trying to analyze the disposition of new missionaries, I would start by saying that we try hard to do everything just right. We want to let the world know that we have come to help them. We have made huge sacrifices to get where we are and have lived all our lives for the purpose of spreading the Word. My thinking was, you give your all for God and He is supposed to bless you accordingly! So in the case of getting this new dog, I figured Schultze would automatically know that I would love and care for him as much as his former master did. But he didn't understand my good intentions. He bit me!

When dear sweet Schultze bit my hand, I was startled. So I hit him. He then jumped up and viciously grabbed hold of my arm. I reciprocated the favor by ramming my fist into the side of his head. He then attacked me, latching on to my other arm. So I kicked him to get him off!

It must have been odd to those who may have caught sight of this outlandish incident — a man and a large dog "duking it out" in a little blue wading pool, with bubbles flying freely! Hopefully we were all alone. At any rate, we had a pretty good tussle for a few very tense moments.

Schultze then realized that I was so mad that I was going to pound him into submission. Sensing my fury, he opted for "Plan B" and beat a hasty retreat.

Desperation can help one accomplish amazing feats. Schultze somehow managed to squeeze underneath the fence and then dashed off down the street. I had to run around to a gate, and when I finally stepped out onto the road he was no where to be found.

I wandered around for about an hour in search of the canine, knocking on doors trying to find someone who had seen him. It slowly occurred to me, the mess I had made of things. I realized that my witness to the people of New Guinea was not all Christ-like. I mean, would Jesus get into a fist fight with a dog?

I dropped to my knees in the middle of the street and told God that I was sorry — sorry for getting angry, sorry for being childish and acting like a fool. I then humbly asked God to bring Schultze back to me. I pleaded with my Father to cause Schultze to both bond with me and feel loved.

Miracles in the Jungle

Still down on my hands and knees, I heard the sound of a branch snapping at the end of the road where the jungle began. Turning around, I couldn't believe my eyes! Like a predator emerging from the forest, there Schultze was. He came running toward me in that wolf-like gait that only a German Shepherd can duplicate.

I couldn't read the expression on his face. Was he going to bite me again?

He trotted right up and let me hold him in a thankful embrace. I wept a bit, grateful that God knows where all His creatures are and that He can communicate with each one!

We went back to the house and finished the bath that had started this whole escapade, without him fighting or resisting me in any way! From then on, he fully submitted to my authority and was my faithful buddy!

Schultze and the village dogs

Did I mention the fact that Schultze was big? Schultze was big! When he stood on his hind legs, he was about the same height as I was (nearly six feet)! You may wonder what kept him from ripping me to shreds when we threw down together in that masculine display of combat.

It was that Schultze had an addiction — called "coconuts."

Beautiful coconut trees grew all over the base, dropping coconuts from time to time.

In American grocery stores, coconuts have already been dehusked. The husk is a two-inch thick cover of very tough, fibrous material protecting the nut within.

Schultze loved to grab these coconuts and rip the husks off! You can't imagine how much strength that requires. There were times, I'm embarrassed to admit, when I would attempt to impress Gail by ripping the husk off the coconut with my bare hands. This usually ended with me straining my arm muscles and with Gail having to rub my sore arms. (So I did it a lot!)

Due to his rogue activity, Schultze's teeth were really worn down and rounded off. That is why he could grab my bare arm and not shred the flesh.

The natives, though, didn't know this, and I never told them our little secret. Schultze would accompany me to the fence gate when visitors wanted to come on base for some particular reason. He'd walk alongside me, looking the person right in the eyes. The place where we stood was at least six inches higher than the visitor's entry outside the fence, and this made our little doggie appear even bigger! If he didn't growl then I knew they were alright and I would let them in. But if he didn't approve of their motives, the look in his eyes would cause them to become disinterested in entering and they would leave in a hurry! He was such an incredible deterrent to crime that I can't recall a single incident in our area while Schultze was present.

However, there was the night the pack of mangy dogs came on base.

My little family and I slept in a small duplex on steel stilts just two feet off the ground. I had constructed a bed for Gail and me that was only 12 inches off the floor. Our outside bedroom wall was primarily a long, screened window.

One night we were awakened by a low growl. Turning my head, I realized that Schultze had his muzzle pressed up against the screen just a couple of feet from where I was lying. Shocked by this, I rose up to investigate. Hearing a ridiculous amount of barking coming from the other side of our yard fence, I grabbed my bow and three arrows with hard rubber bludgeons on their tips and crept quietly out the front door where Schultze was waiting on the porch. I whispered to him, "Follow me and do not attack until I tell you to." Somehow he seemed to understand.

Sneaking up to the gate, a pack of maybe eight very scrawny village dogs came into view. They were leaping and barking ferociously at our neighbor's rabbit cage. I fitted an arrow onto the string and took aim at the largest of the pack. Whap! I nailed him in the chest and sent him rolling and yelping wildly. With one more arrow, I nailed another one before the rest realized what was up. "Attack," I yelled, as Schultze neatly cleared the gate in hot pursuit of the fiendish horde.

He managed to grab one of the slower dogs that hadn't yet made it through the hole they dug under the cyclone fence. He picked it up and shook it. I decided that "to the victor goes the spoils." I turned to go back to bed. It wasn't the first or the last time I had to deal with dogs in the middle of the night.

I would let Schultze have his fun — after all, dogs were a lot easier on his teeth than coconuts!

8 Ifisyu

Walking to my death was something I never thought I would have to do. "Please, Lord, I don't care for my own life, but have pity on my wife and boys."

Ifisyu was a man unlike any other amongst the Iteri people. He was pudgy, almost fat. What is so unusual about someone being chubby? After all, most of us in America could stand to lose a few pounds. But the majority of tribal people that I knew in the jungles of Papua New Guinea were skinny. I'm not saying that you wouldn't find people with a round tummy, but that was usually due to worms rather than too much food and not enough exercise! It was unusual therefore to encounter a chunky person!

Their jungle diet consisted of yams, taro, a variety of tubers, breadfruit, tone fruit when in season, bamboo, sugarcane, an occasional fish, eel or pig, and a substance called sak-sak. Sak-sak is a rubbery gelatin from the sago palm that doesn't taste like anything I've ever experienced in America. It is mostly starch and probably isn't the most nutritious food source known to mankind! Anyway, between the smoking tobacco, the beetle nut (a bit like chewing tobacco) and the primarily veggie diet, there just wasn't a great deal of fat intake. But somehow Ifisyu was fat, probably from just plain sitting around so much! In fact, his nickname in the tribe was "*Lesman*" or Lazy Man.

We had been asked to go to the Iteri tribe and help in the "phase-out" of this work. The Iteri people had been evangelized and the veteran missionaries were either gone or soon to move out. We spent some weeks with one missionary family before they left for Wewak to work in administration. Our job was to focus on the practical needs (math, mechanical, medical) and some spiritual needs to help prepare these people for life on their own.

"Iteri church"

Ifisyu came to me one day with a tropical ulcer on his upper shin. I had a bad feeling about treating him and told him, "I'm afraid to help you because once your leg starts to heal, you'll grow tired of the treatment and decide to wander off into the bush where you can laze around. Then your sore will grow down into your bone and will begin to poison your blood. God's Talk says that the life of the flesh is in the blood, and when the sick grows down into your bone and poisons your blood, then you will come back to me for help — but I will not cut off your leg — and you will die!"

This may sound horribly harsh to the reader, but when one works with tribal people, one learns to be a bit more direct with the patient!

"No, no missionary. I won't shark your talk," the sick man pleaded. "I will hear your talk and obey everything you say. I won't

Miracles in the Jungle

shark the talk, I'll hear it!" (To "shark the talk" simply means to disobey, to not listen, or to avoid the directives of the one in charge.)

"It will be painful and you must come to my house everyday until I say you can go back to the bush," I explained firmly.

"Oh yes, missionary, I will do all that you say. I will hear your talk!" The man was VERY convincing.

Ifisyu was faithful that first week. It was great, almost as if he was a reborn man. He came daily to my house and even endured the painful treatments with little or no protesting. I would scrub the open wound until the greenish brown scab came off, making the sore bleed quite a bit. I then would thoroughly clean the wound with rubbing alcohol and lightly cover the place with some gauze to keep the ever present flies from landing on it and re-infecting it. After each visit, Ifisyu got to sample some tasty food my dear wife would make for being so brave. By the end of the first week, his sore had shrunk from the size of a quarter to an eighth-inch in diameter.

Not only did Ifisyu take pleasure in Gail's culinary giftedness, but he also enjoyed looking at my hunting magazines featuring monster bucks, bears, boars, cougar, elk, moose, rams and mountain goats. He had never seen such amazing creatures as these before! That was the icing on the cake for him. He never grew tired of seeing my two hunting videos of men shooting game with a bow and killing them with only one shot! The bear was a creature that really got his attention. It was always amazing to him that white men could shoot a big boar (bear or pig) with a bow and not get injured by it. The Iteri people have often told me tales and showed me the scars of past hunts where their weapons only wounded and enraged the vicious wild pigs. In fact, one of the very first phrases I learned in the Iteri language was *"Tetiaso, fu wona!"* which means "Watch out, the pig has fight!"

When the second week came, Ifisyu was gone. At first I didn't notice due to the other people we were ministering to on a daily basis. But after three days I asked someone what had happened to Ifisyu.

"He went bush, missionary," Uno told me with a broad smile.

"He gets tired of being near the village," said Tubugi. "He's a lazy man who lets his wife do all the garden work while he lies down and watches."

I remember worrying about Ifisyu going back into the jungle without his sore being fully healed. But then these guys are so tough. They fight sickness and filth from the day they are born. Surely he would be alright and my prediction of sickness going into his bone would be empty. At least that's what I hoped for.

Uno, his wife, and a young man named Afu helped us with the children's ministry. Many of the children ran around with nothing to do all day but to get into trouble. Often they would hang out in groups near our house just watching us. So I decided to work with these Christian young adults, Uno and Afu, to help them see the value of teaching the kids of the village. We had a great time together. We'd gather around and play various games (soccer, kickball, run-pig-run, and freeze tag). We taught the children stories out of the Bible. I showed them how to repair simple equipment. And we even tried to teach some how to play the guitar.

About a month passed with Ifisyu gone — and then it happened.

"Missionary, Ifisyu is dead! Come quickly, he lies in a hut on the other side of the river in the village!" someone yelled from outside my office window.

Now when a person says that someone has died, you must understand that can mean at least three different things. The first kind of "dead" can mean that someone has fainted or has passed out — kind of dead, but not really!

For instance, someone came running one day and told me that my friend Tubugi had died. I ran like a wild man to his house about a mile away in the jungle. When I arrived he was sitting on his front porch rubbing his head. He had bumped his head and fallen down, but clearly he was not dead and certainly not injured very badly. He probably had passed out and someone may have jumped to a wrong conclusion!

The second kind of "dead" is when someone is very sick and they may, in fact, really die.

And then, of course, the third category is when someone truly is dead.

Miracles in the Jungle

Over time I grew reluctant to just drop everything and run when someone had "died." But then there was the day I was mowing the airstrip and someone yelled that our work boy's sister had died. I decided to finish the row I was on, until I got a sinking feeling in the pit of my stomach, so I turned the tractor around and drove straight for the end of the airstrip to investigate. Sure enough, to my horror, there she lay in the middle of the trail, very dead and very pale. I was shocked. At a mere 27 years of age I did not have a clue what to do. People were coming from across the river and looking to me to see my response. I stood there wondering if I was supposed to try to raise her from the dead or what? Talk about feeling helpless.

So this time, when they told me that Ifisyu was laying dead across the river, I ran with all my might. I prayed as I ran, asking God to fill my heart with wisdom to know what to do. I remember wondering in disbelief how it was that the very thing I warned Ifisyu about actually came to pass. I suddenly wished that I had not said anything at all.

Having crossed the river, I encountered a male pig that charged my bare legs. I kicked him with all my strength in a desperate effort to keep him from biting me. It worked; he went squealing off the path and ran under the posts of someone's house.

When I arrived at the hut where Ifisyu was I got a shock. He had been reduced to skin stretched over a skeleton. His leg was rotting and a swarm of bees buzzed around it, eating the flesh. He lay there not quite dead but not saying a word.

I ran the mile back to our house to get advice from the medical station over the radio. The doctor asked me if we had any Chloramphenicol (a very strong antibiotic). We did. He instructed me on how the shot was to be administered and then added, "It will either kill him or kill the infection and help him get well." I wasn't very excited about that prognosis.

Taking the needle, I dashed back across the river to the village and climbed up into the small hut built on stilts. When I administered the large dose of medication, Ifisyu screamed out in pain. I prayed for him and asked that God's will be done. After he settled back down, I expected him to go to sleep. I then returned home.

After telling all to my wife, I sat down to eat some rice, tin fish, and beef crackers for lunch.

While I was still eating, Uno and Afu and one other man came to me.

"Ifisyu died, missionary," Uno said slowly. And then his eyes lit up and so did the faces of the others. "But right before he died, he sat up, smiled, and said, 'Jesus is reaching His arms out for me, and He tells me not to be afraid!' Then he died and his body slumped back to the floor."

Many in the village of Iteri had "hung up their belief" (placed all their trust) in Jesus. It was then that I learned that Ifisyu was one of them.

I stood there not knowing what to think. Then I noticed that the three got very sullen and Uno said, "Missionary, Yesiye is making man-arrows. You must run away."

"What are you talking about?" I asked. "Why should I run away?!"

"Yesiye is going to kill you. You killed his brother Ifisyu and now he is making man-arrows to kill you!"

Yesiye, the chief, was a man that was at my house often. I considered him my friend and also my brother in Christ. I had no idea that Ifisyu was his brother.

"Yesiye and family"

For a moment I just stood there. And then it dawned on me, what would happen to my wife and two small boys? I looked at my Iteri friends, then I started walking down the airstrip toward the village across the river.

"No, missionary, you must not go that way! Yesiye is making man-arrows to kill you!"

I kept walking and then started jogging toward the river, my mind bewildered. I knew only two things: first, I couldn't run away from nor could I fight against the people that God sent me to love; and second, if I was to be killed I didn't want my wife and children to witness it. I would trust in the Lord's plan for my life.

When I was about twelve years old, I was very sad. I didn't feel loved and I lived with so much sorrow in my heart that I wanted to die. As I sat in my closet one morning, pondering putting a rifle to my throat, these words rang crystal clear in my mind: "You are MY workmanship, created in Christ Jesus for good works, which I prepared beforehand that you should walk in them." I thought about that. God was clearly smarter and more powerful than I was. If He in all His infinite wisdom could create such complexity and purpose in the Universe, then surely He could guide me in the purpose for which He created me. It was a major turning point in my life. I put the rifle down and surrendered control of my life to God. I knew then and there that He would lead and direct me.

Many times I have been face to face with death. There was the time I was speeding down the hill on my bicycle. I enjoyed the adrenaline rush of going fast. At the bottom of the hill was an intersection where the highway split into two roads. I looked, saw nothing, and so decided to continue full speed ahead. As I hit the end of the road my bicycle and I violently turned 90 degrees. A pickup truck with a canopy sped by and brushed my arm. I knew in that instant that **I** had not turned the bike and that **God** had miraculously spared my life. It happened many other times in my life, and every time I was reminded to Whom I belonged.

But now it was different somehow. As I walked up the bank on the opposite side of the river, my stomach started to turn sick with emotion. Tears welled up in my eyes. I cried, "I don't care for my own life, but please, Lord, have pity on my wife and boys."

I stumbled forward by myself, blindly trusting in God. This time the male pig saw me and ran. Good thing too, because I wasn't feeling very spry.

When I arrived at Yesiye's house, I couldn't help but notice the intricate barbs on the arrowheads he was carving. The Nakwi, Nimo, and Iteri people all have their own style of carving man-arrows with which to kill enemies. It's weird to think of objects which are crafted to kill you as beautiful, but these were true works of art. I shuddered as I thought of what it must feel like to have arrows like these (arrows with MY name on them) pierce through my abdomen and break up inside me into dozens of jagged pieces.

I offered softly, "Yesiye, friend, I'm here." He looked up from his arrow making with a confused and astonished expression on his face.

As chief of the village, Yesiye was used to having to assert himself to be respected. People had learned to fear him. So for someone to come to him when he was preparing to kill them was unnatural. But now his whole world was being challenged. In the old days a man must be killed to pay back the death of another. But they had accepted *Sisasete* (Jesus) and His ways. The teachings of Jesus were definitely NOT the ways of man — stealing, killing, envy, and retaliation. His teachings COMMANDED His followers to love those who hate them, to forgive, to be kind, to feed their enemy, and to show mercy. Yesiye didn't know what to do.

We stood there staring at each other for some tense moments. Yesiye finally broke down and cried, and I put my arm around his shoulder. There was no one watching that day that I know of except our Savior. I asked him to forgive me and assured him that I loved his brother and tried my best to save his life. I told him what the others had explained to me — how Ifisyu had sat up to embrace *Sisasete* as He came to take him to his home in Heaven.

I didn't have a long talk with Yesiye. I just reminded him of how Jesus wants us to live and I encouraged him that someday we'll get to be in His place where there is no death.

After that, I simply started walking back to my house. I wanted to ask him for the arrows he had made for me — but decided against it!

9 What is a Missionary?

"...As the Father has sent Me, I also send you." John 20:21

The word "missionary" seems to mean many different things to many different people.

To some it is a dreadful image of a stern and pious Westerner in ridiculous khaki garb that goes tromping about the jungles of this earth in search of little dark skinned people with bones sticking out of their noses. This zealot's greatest desire in life is to foist his belief system on poor unsuspecting tribal folks. The image of a peaceful native without a care in the world diligently tending to her garden comes to mind — when all of a sudden out from behind a tree pops a dreaded missionary. Pow! He knocks her to the earth with an enormous, leather bound, giant print KJV Bible and commands her to repent or burn forever in Hell. She struggles to resist his tactics, just wishing that some benevolent anthropologist from the National Geographic Society would come and deliver her from this missionary menace. Oh if only some smart scientific type would come and fill her heart with the hope-filled message of atheism. You know, that wonderful **belief** system in which there is no god — we all just evolved from ape-like creatures which evolved from the primordial soup ponds that naturally formed by the billions of years of rain on the hard rocky crust of the earth! (Sounds scientific, don't you think?) Humans have no worth, after all — we are just a complex mistake of nature with no genuine purpose in life except to live for our own pleasures.

Miracles in the Jungle

For others, a missionary is anyone who attempts to show kindness to someone different than themselves. Maybe a mental image of Mother Theresa comes to mind — just somebody striving to make this world a better place, bravely suffering along side those living in abject poverty.

In America, missionaries put on marriage conferences or travel around an area trying to inspire children to live for God.

Some see teaching English in a foreign nation as missions.

There are those who simply believe that a missionary is one who shares his or her faith with someone else. I've even heard a dear sweet lady say to a group of children, "Be a missionary this week by sharing something nice with one of your neighbors - it could be a popsicle..."

Is sharing a popsicle really what Jesus had in mind when He commanded His followers to go out into all the world and preach the Gospel to every creature? Is His command to make disciples carried out by doing nice things to make this world a better place?

"Missionary"

Our word "missionary" comes from the Latin which means "to be **sent**." The Greek word from which this is taken is "apostolos" (Strongs 652) which means "a delegate, specifically an ambassador of the Gospel, a commissioner of Christ," and it is translated as "apostle, messenger, he that is sent."

Jesus — the first missionary

The Creator of the universe **sent forth** His Son to redeem His creation back to Himself by offering up His only begotten Son in our place! (John 3:16, 17)

"But when the fullness of time had come, God **sent forth** His Son, born of a woman, born under the law, to redeem those who were under the law, that we might receive the adoption as sons." (Galatians 4:4, 5, emphasis added)

In Hebrews 3:1 Jesus is called the "Apostle and High Priest of our confession." He faithfully accomplished the mission on which

His Father sent Him. Jesus lived and walked among us and completely fulfilled His Father's perfect requirements — the law of God. Then Jesus chose men to follow Him, and after giving them authority, He **sent them forth** to proclaim the message in all the earth (Matthew 28:18-20).

The Body of Christ

"And He Himself gave some to be apostles, some prophets, some evangelists, and some pastors and teachers, for the equipping of the saints for the work of ministry, for the edifying of the body of Christ," (Ephesians 4:11.12)

Some say that the apostles were only the original twelve and those who had seen Jesus (Paul and Barnabas) — this is in the strict sense of the word. I believe that in the broader sense an apostle today is one who is selected by God to go forth and establish other local bodies of Christ all over the world in the authority of the original Apostle of our faith — in other words, a missionary. We **all** have the responsibility to share our faith as ambassadors of Christ (2 Corinthians 5:21) — this is evangelism. But some are called to go, being prayerfully commissioned and sent out from their local church.

The Body of Christ is diverse with many gifts. A fully functioning body will have men who pastor the flock (an elder with the heart to shepherd), other elders who administrate and are spiritually mature enough to lead as they are in the Word and in prayer, those who serve the practical needs (deacons), those who sense when things are getting off base with the Word of God (prophets, the bony finger gift), those with the gift of evangelism (soul winners), those with the gift of helps, mercy, hospitality, *and* those who are sent out from the body to plant new churches (missionaries/"apostles").

But do we really need missionaries?

Who would possibly want what we have to give? Aren't they (people separated from the gospel) happy just the way they are? Do we have the right to push our beliefs on others? Don't we have to earn the right to give the gospel — you know, give them some food or something before we ram the Bible down their throats? Do the people in isolated areas need to hear the gospel message, or do they simply need to be left alone?

I traveled to many places during our time in PNG, and I tried always to ask open-ended questions of those I met. On one trip I befriended a man named Tomas. I asked him what life was like when he was a child and this is what he told me:

"When I was young we lived in fear constantly. I and the other children of the village would find places to hide ourselves before the darkness came, so that if our enemies or the evil spirits we feared came in the night to harm us, we wouldn't be found. We did not dare leave the safety of our hiding places to relieve ourselves, but rather we would sleep in our own filth. We were very hungry and very scared growing up. When God's Talk came to us, it changed our lives forever. We no longer feared the spirits of the jungle and we no longer lived like animals."

An old man, who I knew had once been a cannibal, came to my porch one evening to chat with me. I asked him what life was like when he was young. This is what he said:

"Oh Dave, before, before true (long, long ago), when I was young, we Iteri people lived in darkness. You know how the pigs stick their noses into the ground blindly searching for food? That's how we Iteri people were. We danced before the spirits and gave them offerings to give us power over our enemies. We did dances to the spirits to mark out women we wanted to take. If we saw someone's garden, we would steal the food from it. If we saw an enemy we would kill and eat him. If we saw a woman we would rush her and take her. We lived like pigs. We did NOT have the thinkings of a man. Our minds were like the minds of animals. We lived in constant fear of our enemies and also of the spirits in the jungle. But when missionary Brad came and told us God's Talk, the

words burned inside of our stomachs and we knew this is really true talk. And when we hung up our belief in Sisasete (Jesus Christ), our eyes were opened and we were given new minds. Now we live differently. We no longer kill, rape, and steal. We no longer live in constant fear of the spirits. Our eyes are bright and we have the thinkings of a man."

As I talked with these and many other nationals, I couldn't help but wonder what it must be like living without the knowledge that the Creator of the universe loves us and desires a personal relationship with us.

Eddie would go

We once lived for a short time on the island of Maui in Hawaii and while there we kept noticing a bumper sticker with the slogan "Eddie would go." I asked a native of the island what that meant, and he shared this story with me: A boat was in trouble and slowly going down out in the ocean. Upon hearing of this tragedy, Eddie immediately went out to try to rescue the passengers. He was never seen nor heard from again.

The message is: *Eddie would go... how about you?* Do you care so little for the fate of others that you can calmly sit night after night in your Lazy Boy, saddened only by the fact that the batteries in your remote force you to leave the comfort of your chair momentarily? Has God graciously given you anything of value to share with others? (check out Matthew 25:15) Would you leave the comforts of your home and go to those living in darkness, even if it cost you your life?

The day we moved out of our house in the New Guinea jungle, three men from a different village two days hike away arrived and begged me to come live with them. They promised to build us a house, to plant us a garden, and to take care of us. They explained that they too wanted to hear God's Talk and that no one could teach it to them in their own language. They entreated me with intensity. As we left, they rolled on the wet, muddy ground, crying out to us.

This would be a great shame to these men, but they pled pitifully with us to come to them.

Our mission at the time needed us in the capital city to run the guest house. I wondered how it could be — with *so* many Christians in the world — that we have such a lack of missionaries willing to go and proclaim Jesus Christ to those lost without Him. **Would you go?**

10 The Art of Language Learning

Desperation will teach a starving man how to garden!

Some humorous and helpful info for those of you who will become missionaries or for those praying for a missionary overseas

Most people dread the prospect of language learning. After all, you already know how to say what you want to say — it's the other guy that is just too daft to understand, right?!

Your attitude can change drastically, however, when you find yourself caught out in 110 degree weather. You've been busy drinking in the local culture, when suddenly you discover to your horror that the greasy little biscuit thingies you just snarfed down at a roadside stand are wreaking havoc with your innards. I mean to tell you, the streets are crowded and you can't spot a public restroom in this little third world wonderland to save your life! What's worse is the countdown has started, and you're moments away from experiencing a nasty blast off! What I'm trying to say is, **Houston, we have a problem!!!**

Now at that particular bubble in time, wouldn't it be nice to be able to simply ask one of those innocent bystanders where one might go to tidy up a bit? You see, the ability to communicate (using words!) with the thousands around you can make the difference in how the locals will be remembering you for years to come! I can just hear the circle of snickering native folks recalling the foreigner who shamelessly darted about in the midst of the market place doing something resembling a rain dance. A hush had spread over the busy market as everyone present attempted to find meaning in the foreigner's gyrations. Was there a message in his movements? What was he trying so desperately to communicate? And then there was something barely audible resembling thunder, but no dark clouds appeared overhead. Snickering suddenly fell over the masses as all eyes beheld the stilled rain dancer with his very red face. (I know what you are thinking! No, this did NOT happen to me, because I worked hard to memorize the location of every bathroom in town first!)

So with the fear of incorrectly prescribing how to learn a language looming over me, I will attempt to communicate in 10 easy steps how *we* went about language learning.

1. Select someone from the language group with whom you can spend a lot of time and who has a good appetite. Have you ever heard the expression "fattening one up with friendship"? People are less likely to talk about you behind your back when you are feeding them lavishly! What I'm referring to, in essence, is damage control! I had people over quite a bit, and I can assure you Gail's good cooking covered my lack of ability on many an occasion. In fact, I ended up with quite an assortment of eager language experts in a very short amount of time!

2. Try to get someone who doesn't have a lisp or any other speech impediment. How do you know if your local language expert has a speech impediment? You'll know sooner or later, but large crowds gathering around you on a daily basis trying to get you to say certain phrases over and over again is one clue. When they are rolling around on the ground holding their sides with tears streaming down their faces, you may begin to suspect that *your* version of *their* language is a bit off.

3. There is a window of time in which you can and *SHOULD* make all your cute little mistakes. You see, after you've been in a place for four or five years and are still talking like a baby, it is no longer cute

Miracles in the Jungle

to the people around you. I frequently used this to my advantage by addressing people with phrases that sounded like proper greetings but meant something completely different.

For instance, a typical greeting might be, "Ah, you're here are you?" but I would say, "Ah, you've eaten someone today, have you?" This was a particular favorite with guys that I suspected of cannibalism in their past! The people just assumed I was still learning and would smile broadly and shake their head, "Yes, yes." Another joke I played on kids all the time was, "Good morning, crocodile" or "Good day to you, my great grandpa" or "Hello, pretty lizard" or "Greetings, my tin of fish" and many other such silly things. They'd laugh and laugh, thinking it was a great game. They always looked forward to seeing me so that they could try to think up some funny response as well!

One mistake I made, however, came when I was cleaning out the daily bugs from our house for Gail. We lived deep in the jungle in the Iteri tribe and during the night various "friends" in the form of scorpions, spiders, centipedes and huge millipedes would invade our house. I carefully picked up a millipede that must have been at least 10 inches in length. I wanted to show the guys the new phrases I'd learned. Looking through my screen door window, I saw some men standing just outside, including the village chief Yesiye. Opening the door I told them, *"Tetiaso mamai waido"* (watch out, the millipede is here). With a big smile I flicked the gargantuan millipede out from behind my back and tossed it Frisbee-style into the group of scattering men. Unfortunately, the beastly little fellow struck Yesiye right in the chest!

I need to explain something that I was unaware of before this event. You see, I grew up with a discipline device called "a spanking." You commit a crime, you get your swats, and presto, you're back in the ball game of life! But the Iteri didn't know anything about discipline. They would *punish* their children. If a young person was found to be naughty, an adult would grab a millipede with two sticks and squeeze the insect next to the child causing it to spray acid onto the his skin. I had unwittingly picked up dozens of these huge insects without any of them ever biting me or spraying me with their acid. (Makes you wonder how many times God really intervened on our behalf!)

Well anyway, when this bug hit Yesiye in the chest, he dropped his bow, his fist full of arrows, and his shot gun! He plummeted to the ground and lay there screaming and crying. WOW, did I feel stupid, awkward, and embarrassed. I just thought I would show off a little with my new proficiency in their language, but inadvertently I'd caused the chief to have great shame. I quickly turned and darted into the house hoping they would forget my *faux pas*! They did forgive me and nothing was ever said of this afterward.

<u>4. Try as hard as you can to say whatever the people encourage you to try saying</u>. You may feel a little foolish or downright discouraged. Don't! The people love it, as they can laugh and smile and make merry — and inside they are growing to love you. You provide them with lots of entertainment and they are pleased that you are trying so hard to learn THEIR language! Don't pass this up. A little embarrassment now is well worth the long term benefits!

Patrick, an educated national friend of mine, and I used to play a game to help us learn to speak just like people in different parts of the country. As we worked together we would converse with different accents or in different languages that we'd picked up. It was a fun way to pass the time and it ended up saving my life one night.

You see, my family and I spent our first seven months in PNG learning the trade language in an area that had three different dialects. Depending on who I was talking with, I was taught three different ways of saying certain things. It doesn't take a brain surgeon to figure out that everyone wants you to speak just like they do! So I tried really hard to learn the different phrases in *their* version of the language.

The day came when I needed to find a way to get our belongings from the coastal town of Wewak to Maprik. It was my custom to flag down a truck and give them some fuel money for the ride. It was an excellent chance to learn more language and culture and have some crazy adventures. I finally found a truck that was going to Maprik and I boarded. We drove around Wewak, the men claiming they needed to do various things before leaving. But I noticed that the men were a bit edgy. It grew dark and we still hadn't left town. I was becoming concerned that these guys had other things in mind. Finally they explained that they were going to take me for a boat ride and "show me the ocean." I prayed quietly to myself and asked God for wisdom. We got out into the bay about a half mile from shore and then they killed the boat engine. I don't know if they wanted to see if I would become fearful or not, but I was at peace. I don't recall how it happened exactly, but I spoke some of their dialect and they were very surprised at this. They called me their "wantok" (a friendly expression for someone who speaks their language), and promptly took me back to the mission base. I don't want to make more out of this than there really was, but it seems that my ability to speak their dialect saved my skin. For some criminals it's a "notch on their gun" to kill a man, especially a white man.

5. Try eating their food. Just remember that the God Who created the Universe is completely able to bless the food you are given to eat. And the people will love you for it.

A little old woman who may have never taken a bath in her life once handed me a dirty fist full of some nasty kind of meat. I smiled bravely as my insides were doing jumping jacks. I suspected that she had TB and possibly some alphabet soup diseases not yet discovered by western doctors. But then I remembered a scripture about God sanctifying the food that you pray over. (1 Timothy 4:4, 5 — it pays to know the Word of God!) So I gave thanks to God for it and raised it up to Him as a faith offering! I then downed the slimy substance with as much thankfulness as I could muster.

Whether you are given something to eat that you like or something you don't like, give thanks to God and ask Him to bless it. Besides, you don't need enemies at this stage in the game; you'll get plenty of them later on, believe me! And furthermore, it is a common belief (with the exception of Gail) that if you eat the local food, it will somehow help you to be able to speak their language! (Worked for me!)

A side note here regarding eating bugs and other such "tucker" (Aussie for food): When you are in the jungle, hiking hours upon end, basically starving to death, the food you eat becomes very precious to you. I kid you not when I say this,w there are times now that I CRAVE some of the food I used to eat in the jungle. And no, grasshoppers and grubs do *not* taste like chicken!

6. Spend lots and lots of time with the people. I don't know if you are a wall flower or a people person, but if you are in a foreign country you should **NOT** be isolating yourself from the populace. Many people come to a foreign nation with dreams of helping others, but then they encounter the barrier of language. Quickly they discover that learning a language is difficult — challenging — *work* — something that requires focused energy and great effort! I don't know how else to put it — training your mind to think the way other people communicate requires much time spent with them and much discipline.

When one friend of ours couldn't pronounce certain words very well, an unkind native laughed at him. So he decided the next day to stay inside his room and listen to a music CD from back home. Nobody laughed at him. And the next day he decided to battle the evil cards in a game of Solitaire. It was the same story, not a critic to be found. Day after day went by without any interaction with the people. They wondered if he was sick. After all, wouldn't he be outside with them if he could be? Soon a rumor started circulating that he had not really come to be with them. They didn't like him nearly as much as they had at first and they began to question why he was really there. With the people not making this new missionary feel welcome, he started feeling more and more alienated from them and retreated into his bungalow for longer periods of time. It was a short while later that he left PNG to go back home.

Jesus Christ came to be with people. People are problems, but our Savior came to seek and to save the lost.

7. Don't bring too many tribal guys over to eat with you without first telling your wife. Okay, I know what you are thinking. What kind of a nincompoop would be so daft as to bring a bunch of tribal guys over for dinner without telling his wife about it first? I don't want to talk about it now, and I don't appreciate you calling me a nincompoop!

8. <u>Get lots of sleep to rest your weary mind and frazzled emotions</u>. If you are in the habit of inviting natives over without first telling your wife, you'll be doing a lot of sleeping in what they call the "man house." Sleeping out in the community "man house" is not a great way to rest your weary mind and frazzled emotions! Although you will be sure to learn things about the culture that you wouldn't learn anywhere else, guaranteed!

A little side note on "man talk": It might sound really weird, but in New Guinea there is language that is forbidden for a man to reveal to a woman. Men that I spent a great deal of time with would teach me "man talk" when we were camping out in the bush — language that was absolutely forbidden for a woman to ever hear. (Sorry, ladies, I would love to tell you some, but then I'd have to kill you!)

9. <u>Get over the hump!</u> There will come a point when you will have an adequate grasp of the lingo to say pretty much anything you like. But you shouldn't stop there. Keep working to learn new ways of saying things, as you will find that others in the tribe use various other expressions to communicate. Don't make the mistake of becoming a language cripple. Knowing how to say "Missionary want really need find bathroom now" is not the same thing as **knowing the language**.

10. <u>THIS IS THE MOST IMPORTANT ONE: Pray like crazy that God will supernaturally help you to understand the language and culture in which you live</u>. Nothing funny here - desperation **will** teach you how to speak the language! If you have something important to communicate to these people to whom God sent you, you better spend time on your knees beseeching God Almighty for help! He not only knows every language but He also understands the thoughts of everyone's heart. Plus He can save you many years of frustration and heartache. I can't tell you how many times God revealed to me some insight or clue that got me encouraged enough to keep on keeping on. It's a journey, friend, keep pressing forward!

11 The Gospel

*The gospel of Jesus Christ is the power of God
to save everyone who believes.
Paraphrase of Romans 1:16*

The gift of salvation that God offers to all

We all like to receive gifts. Can you imagine the One who gave you physical life, the gift of sight, taste, hearing and touch, offering you another gift? What kind of a gift would He want to give to you? It is the gift of eternal life with Him in heaven.

For the wages of sin is death, but the gift of God is eternal life through Jesus Christ our Lord. Romans 6:23

But how do we receive His gift?

A prison guard asked Paul and Silas, "Sirs, what must I **do** to be saved?" They replied, "**Believe** on the Lord Jesus Christ, and you **will be** saved…" (Acts 16:31 emphasis added)

When I was a little boy my Sunday School teacher told me that all people everywhere are born with a sin nature. It is sin that keeps us from being a part of God's family. It is sin that causes us to commit evil and it is sin that God MUST judge. I learned that hell was the place prepared for those who choose to reject God's offer of His payment for their sin. Hell is a place of eternal torment and utter darkness. What would it be like to be so completely separated from THE Author of Life? Jesus Christ, God's only begotten Son, died and shed His blood to pay the price for our sin. The same God Who made us also made **the only** way we can be forgiven.

I wondered if I too was a sinner. No, I was a *good* person, surely I would be alright. But later that day, I sat on my bed thinking about sin. The Bible said that we have all sinned and fallen short of God's glory (Romans 3:23). It also said that sin spread to all people after Adam sinned (Romans 5:12). Was God's Word wrong? Was I a sinner? Like a flash through my mind I remembered hitting other kids, saying bad words, lying, bragging, taking things that didn't belong to me. I had to admit, even though I was just a kid, I was not without sin and definitely didn't measure up to God's perfect standard. I needed to be forgiven for my sins if I was going to be found innocent by the Great Judge at the end of my life.

After finding my mother I asked her what I could do to be saved. She told me exactly what the Word of God says in the tenth chapter of Romans, verses nine and ten; *"...that if you confess with your mouth the Lord Jesus and believe in your heart that God has raised Him from the dead, you will be saved. For with the heart one believes unto righteousness, and with the mouth confession is made unto salvation."*

"Dear God," I prayed, "please forgive me for my sin and make me Your child. I believe in Your Son Jesus to take away my sins." I meant it with all my heart back then and I am still trusting only in Him today! Jesus Christ IS my righteousness, I have none apart from Him.

Long ago, God sent a man named Philip to an official of a queen. This royal official was reading the fifty-third chapter of Isaiah as he rode along in his coach. He didn't understand who he was reading about and so God sent Philip to explain the scriptures to him.

After hearing the gospel (that Christ died for our sins, was buried and rose again from the dead) this man realized that Jesus Christ was the very same person he was reading about in Isaiah. He wanted to receive God's pardon and be baptized immediately. In Acts 8:37, Philip tells him, "If you believe with all your heart, you may" (be baptized into the family of God). Then the man cried out, **"I believe that Jesus Christ is the Son of God."**

You need only to repent of your sin (agree with God that you have broken His law) and believe on the Lord Jesus Christ, trusting in Him alone to save you.

"Nor is there salvation in any other for there is no other name under heaven given among men by we must be saved." Acts 4:12

"But as many as received Him, to them He gave the right to become children of God, to those who believe in His name:" John 1:12

"These things I have written to you who believe in the name of the Son of God, that you may know that you have eternal life, and that you may continue to believe in the name of the Son of God." 1 John 5:13

Are you fully trusting in Jesus Christ to save you? Have you confessed Him to others? Will you obey Him by being identified as His follower in public baptism? Will you share this good news with others?